WOMEN OF THE BIBLE.

BY

CHARLES ADAMS.

EDITED BY DANIEL P. KIDDER.

New-York:
PUBLISHED BY LANE & SCOTT,
FOR THE SUNDAY-SCHOOL UNION OF THE METHODIST EPISCOPAL CHURCH,
200 Mulberry-street.
JOSEPH LONGKING, PRINTER.
1851.

INTRODUCTION.

In this book, the author has sought to contemplate woman precisely as the inspired pen has represented her, so far as she has arisen to view in the divine history of God's providential and gracious dispensations to mankind, and so far as that pen may have sketched more didactically her true position and duties.

In pursuance of this plan, careful attention has been given to all the more prominent female characters of the Holy Scriptures, and to whatever lights and shades the unerring pen has left upon their names for the instruction of posterity. Of this department of the divine Book, as of all the rest, may it be said, that it was given by inspiration of God, and is profitable for doctrine, for reproof, for correction, for instruction in righteousness, that the child of God may be perfect. The author deems it just to himself to add, that in attempting to throw himself back amid Scripture characters and Scripture times, he has aimed to keep his eye steady upon recorded facts and incidents, and has forborne, as he hopes, all undue license of the imagination, and all those dreams of which it may be said that "there is no light in them." He has endeavored to write a sober and faithful book—such as, in its plan and execution, in its sentiment and diction, shall do no harm, and may accomplish some good. He is not disposed to conceal, that whatever other benefit may arise out of his humble effort, he has hoped, by these brief sketches concerning various interesting characters of the Bible, to attract the eyes of his fair readers more intently toward that blessed volume, and the priceless treasures of wisdom and knowledge therein contained.

That these aims will insure the approval of the good and virtuous, the author entertains no doubt. To what extent the means he has used for the accomplishment of his object are pertinent and promising, is herewith respectfully submitted to their candid judgment.

CONTENTS.

WOMEN OF THE BIBLE.

Eve.

ALAS for her who was the first and eldest of her sex! Mournful and sad are the associations that cluster around her name. We think of deception, and of the hateful deceiver. We think of the birth of sin,—and the flight of innocence, holiness, peace, and love, from this new-created and beautiful world. We think of paradise lost, on which the sun and stars shall shine no more. We think of the fearfulness of the divine curse—of pain and sorrow—of dying and of death. It is true, there arises a bow upon the awful cloud. There is a whisper of hope heard amid the thunders of this earliest storm of earth. Under that cold and long eclipse, and amid the heaving, and crushing, and dying, and those "signs of woe that all is lost," may be seen a gleam of holy light coming from afar. Yet the mystic ray reveals no release from the fatal wreck. It tells that death has arrived—that paradise must henceforth be sought in other worlds, and that, too, by long and painful struggles with the enemy of righteousness.

Her more thoughtful sons and daughters will forbear to curse their first mother. The blame they attach to her will be mingled with pity. Yet no one can compute the sorrow—the deep, heart-breaking sorrow, that has been felt by millions in remembrance of her fall. They have thought of her as, in the days of her innocence, she stood the loveliest ornament of a lovely world,—whose beauty and grace were such as that the inspired pen forbore, as of the forms of angels, to portray them; who was ushered, a perfect being, upon a scene of perfect happiness; whose guiltless bosom swelled with naught save peace, and joy, and love; across whose delighted vision there flitted no images of sin, or grief, or drooping sickness, or noisome graves; whose rejoicing spirit was as unconscious as the laughing infant's, of direful changes, or dying scenes, along the illimitable future; whose form of beauty, and flowing tresses, and every line and feature of enchanting gracefulness, were fashioned for immortality; who looked up upon her husband, and, reading there at once the image of God and the counterpart and companion of herself, leaned toward him with a love ineffable, and hailed there the charm of her soul and the completion of her blessedness; who, side by side with him, as they roamed amid those groves, held long communings with superior beings, and listened to the songs of angels swelling afar, and heard the footsteps of the Lord God, and, in their innocence, were not afraid.

The heart weeps as it meditates that such bliss as this should, all suddenly, be crushed forever; that the fair garniture of the virgin earth should, as in a moment, be displaced by thorns and briers, and all unsightly and noxious things. O! there are tears for the cloudless morning of that day—the day when sin and death were let loose along this world—when beauty, formed for eternal bloom, began to fade, and the image of heaven was effaced from the human spirit—and the serpent first nestled there—and the sting of woe first entered the soul—and tears of bitterness first fell—and the smiles of the Eternal were withdrawn, to be replaced by his frown and curse, for the sake of man. The mind is reluctant to look upon the sad afterpart. Where goes she who, just now, was fairer and happier than since have been all the daughters of men? Is she driven away from that garden of beauty and of safety, to return no more? Hears she some dreadful note assuring her of "sorrows greatly multiplied?" And retiring from her early home—the home of unsullied peace—do other suns now light upon her? Do frightful storms beat upon her head? Does she grow weary and faint? Does she pine in sickness? Is she fading into age? Her husband, also; is he greatly changed? Amid all, does she remember the days of her fair morning of existence? Does every pain, and every discordant sound, and frowning look, and fading brow, and every noise of strife and murder, and each venomous and poisonous breath, and all dark and mournful prospects, and every ghastly dying scene; do they forever whisper of the joys that were hers, when away in that garden of innocence and unfading happiness?

The time spent by our first parents in a state of innocency is not known, although there are indications that it was but brief. The fatal facility of Eve's deception impresses us that she had but begun to taste of life; that the world to which she was introduced was still rising before her under aspects of novelty and freshness, and awaking within her breast a curiosity as childlike as it was intense. Then, again, she had no offspring while yet unfallen. This fact, taken in connection with the command of God to our first parents in reference to posterity, is almost, if not quite conclusive that their days of innocence were few indeed. And further still. Cain and Abel, though born after the fall, had come to manhood, and Abel had been murdered before the birth of Seth; at which time their parents were one hundred and thirty years of age. Considering the protracted youth and manhood of the race at that period, it seems fair to infer, therefore, that those years had almost all elapsed since the transgression. After the fall, we trace our first mother to the birth of Seth; from which period she is not named, and there is no record of the duration of her life. We may, however, very nearly identify her life with that of her husband;

and as he still lived for hundreds of years subsequently to the birth of Seth, and sons and daughters were born to him, we may count his history, so far as given, to have been that of his wife. They both lived long—very long, and then—*they died!*

There is unfathomable—awful mystery in the catastrophe of Eve. Let not her daughters be too inquisitive and too censorious respecting her. Beware that ye charge not God foolishly, nor cherish a reproachful thought touching his inscrutable Providence. The solemn voice from that great disaster whispers rather, Beware of the ancient Serpent! He is still abroad; his beguilings have not ceased, and his devices are many; his darts fly in every direction; he seeks whom he may devour; and millions are led captive by him at his will. Forget not that naught, save One, can bruise him under your feet. With the promised and great Deliverer, there is safety and eternal victory. Away from him, there is certain capture and ruin.

Sarah.

SARAH, who was originally named Sarai, was the daughter of Terah, was born in Ur of the Chaldees, and became the wife of the illustrious Abraham. Subsequently to their marriage, and by revelation to Abraham, the family, consisting of her husband, her father, and Lot, emigrated to Haran, where Terah ended his days, at the age of two hundred and five years. After his death, Abraham and Lot again removed westward, and went to Canaan, which was then in possession of the original race inhabiting that region of country. Here Abraham was favored with special and repeated revelations from God; was promised that the land to which he had come should be given to his posterity, and he became great in wealth and power.

Sarah appears to have been a woman of extraordinary beauty of person, which she retained to a very late period of her life; so that, at ninety years of age, she attracted the attention and love of Abimelech, king of Gerar; he being unaware of her relation to Abraham. At the age of seventy-five years, having relinquished the idea of bearing children, she sought, according to a usage not unknown to those times, to gain posterity by proxy. Accordingly she gave to her husband as a wife her bondmaid Hagar, who became the mother of Ishmael. At the very advanced age of ninety, however, Sarah also, and by an extraordinary providence, gave birth to a son, who was Isaac, and heir of the special and Divine promises which had been made to Abraham. After the birth of her son, Sarah survived about thirty-seven years, and died at Kirjath-arba, afterwards Hebron, aged one hundred and twenty-seven years.

The character of Sarah, so far as portrayed on the page of revelation, is marked, as is natural, by alternate light and shade. She is not without prominent excellences, and hers is recorded among the honorable names of sacred story. At the same time, we may discern, even in Sarah, the marks of our fallen nature; some of those indisputable tokens that whisper to us of human imperfection.

We feel little admiration, for example, of her arrangement with respect to her husband and Hagar. We accord to her, it is true, the usual indulgence allowed in consideration of custom—the lack, in that early period, of Divine communication—and, perhaps, some other circumstances. Yet we can hardly refrain from discerning in her at this period, and in this incident of her history, a deficiency of that patience which is so beautiful a characteristic of the sex. We seem to detect a want of that pious and graceful submission to the will of Providence, so essential to woman,—and of that commendable faith in the great Father, which we are assured she was enabled to exercise in after years. Had not God, long before, and more than once, spoken to her husband by special and heavenly messages? Had not that husband already become great and powerful? And was it a secret to the companion of Abraham, that to him was promised, by the One who cannot lie, a posterity that, in multitude, should vie with the stars of heaven, and that in his seed all the kindreds of the earth were to be blessed? With these Divine assurances in memory, was it necessary for her to arise and forestall the movements of sacred Providence? Was she called to put forth her hand? Did any voice from heaven suggest in her ear that she must hasten, and, at all events, make sure of the fulfillment of that word which stands though heaven and earth depart? Was it not her province, rather, to "hope and quietly wait?" What pity that, in that hour, there occurred not to her mind what an angel, in after time, inquired of her, saying, "Is anything too hard for the Lord!" Thus had it told for her reputation for wisdom as well as for piety, in the eyes of the millions of every age of time to whom the name and history of Sarah were destined to be familiar. And it is not all recited to us—a mere hint or two are given—of what were the domestic broils; the frequent and numberless vexations; the sad spoiling of earthly sunshine, that commenced with Abraham's new and unnatural espousals, and ended—we know not when. O! there is a time to act, and a time to cease from our own works. There is a time to move forward and achieve priceless victories, and a time to stand still and see the salvation of God. And she who, like the daughters of Israel, watches with Moses the rising and reposing of the pillar of cloud and fire—shall not fail, with Miriam and her sisters, to sing that "the Lord hath triumphed gloriously."

All the severity of Sarah toward her bondmaid, both at the first, when Hagar fled from her face, and long afterwards, when she was driven into exile with the consent of the weary and weeping husband—all this we look for, as being an incident of the tale as true to nature, as it is unhappy for the reputation of the chief actress in this scene of sadness. Gentleness and pity dwell with goodness, and with the faith that makes not haste, and with the love that suffereth long and is kind. Shut these away from the female heart, and no marvel if there be envy and contention; yea, every evil work.

But there are brighter and fairer features toward which the hand must not fail to point, that would portray correctly the beautiful consort of Abraham. She was not without blemish; yet was she graceful in mind as well as in person. More tokens than one go to mark her as belonging to the most distinguished of her sex, and in many respects a fit companion of one of the greatest men of this world's history. For, is it not fair to inquire as to what that woman must have been, whose influence over a man like Abraham, was what her influence was? In almost every aspect, her husband was superior to most others. Great in physical might, he, with his own household, rushed after and subdued the kings and their hosts. Great in soul, he spurned the rich offer of the prince of Sodom, and passed over to Lot the little matter of assigning their respective earthly possessions. Great in precedence, he was the ancestor and father of the faithful. Great in dignity, God and angels often conversed with him. Great afterwards in heaven, Abraham, Isaac, and Jacob have certainly long been there. As we meditate, then, "how great this man was," we may meditate, also, the greatness of her whom he evidently, with all his greatness, profoundly respected, as well as dearly loved. We hazard nothing in writing, that the woman, whom a man like Abraham loved beyond all others for so many years—whose opinion of her attractiveness was such as that he sometimes deemed it dangerous to be known as her husband—who, when at last she slept, bowed his aged and dignified form, and mourned and wept over "his dead,"—still his, though dead,—this woman, surely, can hold no mean place among her sex, and we wonder not that, long centuries after she retired from the world, the hand of inspiration assigned to her name a conspicuous place upon the list of those who, in olden time, believed God, and it was counted to them for righteousness.

Who has not sometimes roamed, in imagination, amid the scenes of patriarchal simplicity and beauty? Has never my fair reader, upon some sultry summer day, trod thoughtfully within the groves of Mamre, and reclined beneath the shady oaks hard by those spacious and graceful tents? At the opening of those lofty and ample folds, and almost facing thee, sits a man of a hundred years; and who has, once and again, talked, face to face, with God. It is a form of surpassing dignity,—erect and strong as when, in other years, he dealt relentless ruin among the conquerors of the plain. Locks hoary, yet pure and beautiful, curl over his shoulders, and a beard of snowy brilliancy reposes upon his bosom,—his eye, large and tranquil, is looking forth upon the magnificence of glorious summer,—or turned upward, now and then, toward the home of the faithful,—or closed, at intervals, as the mind meditates upon remembered scenes, and calls up again unearthly and enchanting voices that used to breathe into his ear exceeding great and precious promises.

On a sudden, those eyes are fixed; the visage becomes prolonged and direct; the whole form leans forward, as with unusual earnestness. Turning your eye in the same direction, and three men are approaching, "if it be lawful to call them men." They came from a far country, and the patriarch is running to greet them, and his noble form is already bowing lowly toward the ground in profoundest obeisance. The greetings cease, and the hospitalities proceed.

But where is Sarah? Just where we would wish to find her, filling the place she is expected to fill, acting the part assigned to her to perform, and realizing to thine eye the obedience, activity, skill, modesty, and dignity of a genuine princess of her times, a worthy companion and friend of one of the chief nobility of earth, and a lovely daughter of her God. Obedience, for her hand is as that of him who directs; activity, for how soon are all things in readiness; skill, for under her superintendence a dish is made ready, of which angels eat; modesty and dignity, for thou, in all this time, and amid all these personages, hast not discovered her, while even the guests are inquiring, as if in wonder, "Where is Sarah?" "Behold, in the tent," is the response; and such it should have been. Would not a more noisy or ostentatious lady—one of more bustle, but of less skill—of more words, but of less dignity and grace—would she not have been seen or heard amid all those hospitable preparations? But there is no confusion—no exposure—no complaint. There is no being "cumbered about much serving." All is order, as well as dispatch—propriety, as well as efficiency. "She is like the merchant ships—she bringeth her food from far. She riseth also while it is yet night, and giveth meat to her household, and a portion to her maidens. Her husband is known in the gates, when he sitteth among the elders of the land."

Of the latter Dispensation, as well as of the former, inspired fingers pointed back to Sarah; and two apostles, under two aspects of exceeding beauty, have registered her name. Paul presents her in the celebrated galaxy of the ancient believers—one of those who obtained a good report through faith, and that compose the great cloud of witnesses beholding from their spheres of light the progress of successive generations of the Christian combatants, as they run up the path of life. Peter presents her as the lovely woman and companion, discarding exterior adorning, and coveting the adorning of the heart, the ornament of a meek and quiet spirit, being in subjection, in the appropriate sense, to her husband, observing toward him the most respectful address and the most exemplary deportment. Paul records her dutifulness to her God; Peter, that to her husband. Paul writes her a believer; Peter, a well-doer also. Paul shows her a saint, looking upward; Peter represents her a saint, forbearing, amid her heavenly visions, to step aside from the proprieties of life. Paul exhibits her as an exemplar for believers; Peter, as the mother of the daughters that do well. The one tells you of her hand being in God's; the other, that, her hand being there, she was not afraid with any amazement.

Lot's Wife.

"Arise, take thy wife," said the angels to Lot, as they urged him away from the city devoted to destruction. Her *relation* only is noticed, and neither her name nor those of her daughters appear upon the inspired page. Of her origin, also, we have no information; and the angelic announcement quoted above, is the first allusion to her in the sacred Scriptures. It appears quite probable that she was a native of Sodom, and became united to Lot after his commencing to reside in that wicked and ill-fated city. When the hour of judgment had come, and while Lot still lingered, the angel men are represented as laying hold upon his hand, and upon the hand of his wife, and upon the hand of his two daughters, the Lord being merciful to him, and they brought him forth, and set him without the city, and said, "Escape for thy life! Look not behind thee—neither stay thou in all the plain. Escape to the mountain, lest thou be consumed." But as they fled from the city, his wife looked behind her, and became a pillar of salt.

A single melancholy allusion is made to her in the New Testament, and by the lips of Christ. As he instructs his disciples touching their flight from the impending ruin of Jerusalem, and warns them, as their flight commences, against returning to their houses for the purpose of taking any of their effects with them, he very naturally refers back to the destruction of Sodom, and to the conduct of her who, as she fled from the city, "looked behind her." "Remember Lot's wife," is the concise and significant warning; and such is the only use for which her name is adduced. She is not recalled, like Sarah, as an example of faith, but is pointed to as a beacon of warning. She is not, like Anna, produced as an illustration of looking to God always, but rather as representative of those who, at times at least, look another way. She had not the promptness of Deborah, as she assures Barak, "I will arise and go with thee;" but she lingers, and hesitates, and pauses. She did not, as did the apostle, press toward the mark; but, as he did not, she remembered the things which were behind. Nor did she, like Mary, have respect to angel voices; but rather, like Sapphira, she listened to the suggestions of covetousness. It was not sufficient that a divine messenger should assure her of the destruction behind,—she must look if it certainly be so.

Yet was it not natural? That city had been her home, perhaps from infancy. Hers was, doubtless, no mean residence there, for her husband was princely in his possessions. There, too, were some of her dear children, whom, as she fled, she had been compelled to leave behind her. Must they, also, be lost in the threatened destruction? Then, again, what would she do in the future? Whither was she flying? Would she find another home, or would she be cast forth—a forlorn exile—to pass her slight remnant of life in poverty, suffering, and weeping?

We marvel not that she "looked behind her." All the natural sentiments of her heart prompted her to such an act. Yet should she not have consented. There are times when the soul must rein itself up to a desperate effort,—when a momentary yielding to natural impulses, or a slight wandering of the eye, or a single word or act of indiscretion, leads on to consequences affecting the destiny and happiness of a life. Especially is disregard of an express injunction of Divine authority pregnant with the most imminent danger. If a heavenly voice whisper, "Look not," then is the time to beware. No matter whether the interdicted vision be of the wine sparkling in the cup, or seductive forms stealing away the heart from God, or terrestrial bowers of beauty too often preferred to heaven, or golden wedges and garments of magnificence captivating the affections, or even home, dear home, where linger those we love better than life—look not on them—one or all of them—if such be God's bidding. Restraining thine eye, may be as if it should be plucked from its socket; thy right hand pointing forever heavenward, may be to thee as though cut off and cast from thee; pressing always, and to the last, after God's leadings, may be as if one should "die daily;" yet let thine eye look right on, and thine eyelids straight before thee; tarry not in all the plain; but fly, for thy life, toward the city and mount of everlasting safety.

Rebecca.

REBECCA is not without fame in sacred story. She was grand-daughter of Nahor, Abraham's brother, and sister of Laban, the father of the wives of her son Jacob. She was highly beautiful in person; and to this were added much simplicity and loveliness of manners, a sprightly action, a graceful hospitality, and, with some important exceptions, a pious trust in the God of providence. On the arrival of Abraham's messenger, sent to procure a wife for Isaac, Rebecca was divinely designated to him as the suitable person for so distinguished a connection; and with the approbation and blessing of her father's house, and accompanied by her nurse and waiting-maids, she cheerfully bid adieu to her home, was conducted to Hebron, the residence of Isaac, and became his wife. This marriage, we may infer, was eminently happy; for Isaac was thus consoled after his mother's death; and such was his love for Rebecca, that, during her life, we do not hear of him, as of Abraham and Jacob, that he allied himself to any other wife. As a companion, she was probably devoted, capable, and answering, in an eminent degree, all the wishes of her husband; and "living faithfully together," no reason existed for any of those matrimonial difficulties which arose so naturally in the families of his father and his son. The whole history of Isaac, indeed, impresses us that he was a man of a gentle, meditative, and quiet spirit; seeking to cultivate peace with all men. At the same time, the Lord of providence gave him great prosperity; endowing him with princely possessions inherited from his illustrious father, while, from the genial influences of an eastern soil and clime, there were added to him the brilliant harvests of an hundred-fold. Amid all his sources of happiness, his beautiful and accomplished Rebecca was, we may believe, the crowning gem,—adding a charm unutterable to all the walks of his earthly pilgrimage, and contributing her quiet, yet powerful influence, in promoting the dignity and peace of a long and tranquil life.

When, or at what age she died, is not recorded. We do not hear of her in life after the departure of Jacob to Haran; at which time her husband was at least a hundred years of age. As Isaac survived eighty years beyond that period, and as there is no record of his being married a second time, it may be presumed that Rebecca also lived to a good old age. Her sepulchre was in the field of Machpelah, purchased by Abraham as a burying-place. "There they buried Isaac and Rebecca his wife."

As we review the history of Rebecca, there is much in the picture that interests and captivates us. We love to think that she was beautiful, and "very fair to look upon." This was doubtless so, however difficult it may be to realize the glory that so long since passed away. We need not doubt that graceful and attractive forms were moving here in old and buried years; and there is sadness in the thought that they have drooped and faded, while the admiration and love which they inspired are also hushed forever. Yet such are we. The fashion of this world, as the ever-changing scenery of the opera, passeth away. So beauty, now blooming as Rebecca's bloomed, will, like hers, decay, and, long before this passing century shall be finished, will have disappeared as the glorious bow upon the cloud of yesterday. A dear and loved possession is that of personal beauty—the perfection of material excellence—if, indeed, it be lawful to call that material, with which the intellectual and the spiritual are so sublimely blended. Yet it tarries not. The "human face divine" puts off its brilliancy, and fades, that it may bloom elsewhere in immortal loveliness.

Beauty of form and feature is more than doubly beautiful, when associated with gracefulness of mind and character. Such were Rebecca's charms. Nothing can surpass the delicious pencilings of that first interview between Abraham's servant and the blooming Syrian maid. As the messenger prays, a damsel is in his thoughts. While yet speaking, a damsel, as if lighting down from above during his prayer, appears before him, and the sign he asked is given. She has filled her pitcher with water, and is returning from the well. "Give me to drink, I pray thee, a little water of thy pitcher!" "Drink, my lord, and I will draw water for thy camels also." Such was the respectful and sweet response of the maid, as with equal promptitude and grace she suited the action to the word. Meanwhile the stranger, in wonder and in silence, ponders the scene before him;—and He who had just now heard his prayer, assured him that the being, concerning whom that prayer was offered, was moving before his eyes. Inquiries and explanations proceed; hospitalities are proffered in the house of Laban; the important message is opened; all arrangements are considered and finished; all, save one. "Rebecca," said they, "wilt thou go with this man?" "I will go," she answered, and thus decided her earthly destinies.

What indescribable beauty and simplicity are here! What implicit trusting in the God of providence! How prelusive is this whole scene, of singular and illustrious consequences! How indicative of a Heaven-appointed and Heaven-approved happiness!

We should note here, too, the sublimity that may be attached to any hour of human history. One day, a sweet and artless girl is rejoicing within one of the dwellings of the city of Nahor. At evening, she goes out, as was customary with the daughters of the city, to bring water from the neighboring fountain. The sun is sinking gradually into the great western sea, and soft airs are breathing along the far-reaching plains of Padan-aram. A stranger is near the fountain, and God is listening there; and his great hand is leading, step by step, and in every accent of her lips, that beautiful and happy maid. In all that day, she dreamed not of the evening colloquy; and as she drew those cooling waters for the refreshment of the stranger, it occurred not once to her how that her very acts and words were all pointing her to forthcoming and distinguished happiness. This evening, she is cheerfully acting her part in the duties of her father's house. Yet, as she moves, an unseen hand is upon her, touching the springs of great and sublime events, and moving the keys of untold destinies. To-morrow, Rebecca is on her way to become the wife of Isaac—a mother in Israel—a link in the golden chain that should reach to the Messiah of God. Gentle reader, walk softly! Place thy frail hand within the hand that is almighty. Thine own prayer, and the prayer of the stranger, despise not; for God is the great Arbiter—and he is listening!

Would there were no shade upon the history of Rebecca! Would that she had never withdrawn her eye from the Divine pointing, nor ventured, with rash step, to tread unhallowed ground! Her favorite son seems likely to lose the principal blessing within the gift of his father. How shall so great an evil be averted, and the dew of heaven, and the fatness of the earth, and all abundance and authority, crown and adorn her beloved Jacob? If such be God's ordinance, can he not bring it to pass? Needs he the rash fingerings of human frailty, to help out his great designs? Especially, does he beckon for the dark steppings of deceit and guilt for the unfolding of his glorious plans? The decisive day is come; the day when the soul of the patriarch confers its selectest blessing. Esau is abroad with his bow, in joyous pursuit of the desired repast that is to precede the promised benediction. Meanwhile, dark words and deeds are passing in the house of Isaac. A spirit of darkness is invoked, to waken light and joy. A jewel, rich and beautiful, rises on the sight; and secured it must be, though the serpent shall be roused to seize it where it lies, and sting to the quick the hands that receive it from his fangs. O! where now was the trust of the good Abraham, who would follow no hand but God's, and that, too, though his hand might seem to urge to tragedy and death! Could not the same voice that preserved Isaac from dying on Moriah, deter him now from giving a wrong direction to the blessings of his father Abraham? How rare is faith on the earth! And if, to-day, her slender hand takes hold upon the great arm, no wonder if, to-morrow, that hand be shattered, and nothing remain but tempests, and tossings, and ruin.

Rebecca sins;—and sin, when it is finished,

bringeth forth death. At once, we hear of hatred where love was; and murderous threatenings are whispered along those once peaceful halls;—and there are dreams of blood—and fears that have torment—and dark anticipations—and sad parting scenes. "Upon me be thy curse, my son!" Alas for such an assumption! Who shall bear another's curse? Now trouble comes. That darling son becomes an exile, to save his life. That fond mother must send him from her presence; and whether she ever sees him again, history is silent. We hear of his hailing his father in after years, but thenceforth there is the silence of death as to Rebecca. There is no voice to speak of her again, telling how long she lived, or when or where she died. Jacob, indeed, once lisps her name; but it is when the damps of death are on his brow; and he only speaks of her as—buried!

Yet hope for Rebecca. Respect her sorrows, as she weeps over the sad absence of her beloved child. Doubt not her penitence before her God, and his forgiveness through the promised Seed. Be there smiles for her dying hours; when the Heaven-destined Isaac leaned over her who was the joy of his life, and pointed her away to the rest of the weary. Joy to the mingled dust, where "they buried Isaac and Rebecca." It shall rise again, one day, in forms more beautiful by far than ever roamed amid the groves of Beersheba, or bloomed by the fountains of Haran.

Leah and Rachel.

LEAH and Rachel were the daughters of Laban, and nieces of Rebecca; and became the wives of her favorite son, Jacob, after he emigrated to Padan-aram. Rachel was the first of her father's family whom Jacob saw after his arrival, and he appears to have been immediately captivated by her beauty. On his introduction to her father, and after the space of a month, he proposed to serve him seven years for the hand of Rachel, and the proposal was accepted. The seven years seemed to Jacob "but a few days, for the love he had to her." At the end of the specified time, however, the elder sister, Leah, was secretly led to his bed instead of Rachel, and seven more years were enjoined by the deceitful and rapacious Laban upon Jacob, in order to the possession of his beloved Rachel.

Thus, in violation of nature's wise and perfect laws, Jacob became at once involved in the perplexing condition of bigamy; and, which might appear one of the most melancholy forms of this unnatural position, two sisters disputed with each other for his affections and smiles. That their common relation to Jacob exerted a highly deleterious influence upon their sisterly relations and affection, we might very safely infer, while the brief incidents of their history sufficiently corroborate such a suspicion.

What nicely-balanced advantages, and what extra-human goodness and forbearance, must combine to insure, under such circumstances, even ordinary tranquillity in the domestic circle! In the case before us, there appears a certain equalizing and opposition of considerations, which may be regarded as providential. Rachel was the more beautiful; Leah, the more fruitful: the latter advantage, according to the sentiment of the people and times, being fully equivalent to the former. If the charms of Rachel won upon the heart of her husband, the piety of Leah could not fail to command his esteem. If Rachel was beautiful, she was yet forward and grasping; if Leah was plain, she was also retiring and submissive. With all the personal attractions of the younger sister, she was, at times, impatient and imprudent; and, on one occasion, at least, exhibited herself as highly unreasonable and blameworthy. The elder sister, on the other hand, impresses us as evincing a grateful spirit for blessings received, as well as a becoming forbearance at any ungraceful neglect on the part of one from whom she rightly conceived that she deserved a more respectful and affectionate bearing. If there were beauty and favor in the tent of Rachel, there were honor and dignity in that of her sister; and if the former might assure herself of her superior personal power over her husband, the latter might point to her blooming progeny, and, like the heroic mothers of an after age, exclaim, "These are my ornaments!"

It becomes us, indeed, to speak gently and cautiously of the two wives of Jacob. Place man or woman in a position varying from that designed by the God of nature and of providence, and no marvel if there be derangement and confusion in the result. There are beautiful simples, which, if brought into certain combinations, produce but deformity; and, in human society, there have often existed alliances as unharmonious as they were unphilosophical, and working out results as awkward and unsightly, as the individuals concerned were, in their separate capacity, lovely and hopeful. I have loved to contemplate the daughters of Laban apart from their common relation to the son of Isaac. Before ever they saw the stranger from afar, it is easy to imagine that, as associates, they were lovely and pleasant in their lives. Whether within doors, concerned with their simple domestic duties, or abroad with their father's flocks, amid the rich and sunny pastures of Padan-aram, we think of them only as one in affection as well as in occupation. The voice of sprightly mirth full often echoed through those chestnut groves; and songs, breathed upon delicious voices, and accompanied by the tabret and the harp, were heard hard by where blissful Eden bloomed in its glory. Were they not sisters then? And sisters should they always have continued, and forborne to dispense with a relation so interesting and innocent, that they might assume another so incongruous and unnatural as to have always remained nameless. Rivalry, on the part of two persons, for the affections of a third, must always be deemed unfortunate and unhappy. Especially melancholy is this state of things when existing with two sisters, born and reared beneath the same roof, and partaking, from infancy, in the same joys and sorrows. And then if, yet further, we conceive such rivalry to be, not the mere transient cloud passing onward, to leave again unbroken the smiling rays that were, for a moment, intercepted—but rather the gloom of a life; a cold and long eclipse, that shall be succeeded only by the shadow of death;—contemplating prospects like these, we are prepared for even graver difficulties than what are written of the wives of Jacob.

Laban, the prime mover, as it respects the unhappy position of his daughters, will be pronounced by all generations as a man whose folly was surpassed only by his meanness. Why urge the gentle Leah to the arms of one who never asked for her? Why not, like a man, inform Jacob, right early, of that custom which was pleaded in excuse for such a proceeding? When an alliance was in prospect, as happy perhaps as was ever formed, why interpose thus lawlessly and absurdly, and spoil the earthly happiness of those two lovely daughters? Why take those innocent and happy sisters, that had ever sympathized, and place them against each other for a life struggle—and, from sisters, shape them into rivals; and in bosoms where mutual love and good-will had been wont to reign, there kindle up the tormenting fires of jealousy, strife, and hatred? Mean man! Shameful violator of all good faith, and unnatural murderer of thine own children's peace!

"Jacob loved Rachel." Ay,—and Rachel should have been the wife of Jacob,—and she alone. He sought no other,—wished no other; and had he been permitted to wed freely the one he loved, their happiness had vied with that of Isaac and Rebecca, and the dignity of their union should have equaled that of Abraham and Sarah. Rachel would have been equally beautiful, and more excellent, as well as more honorable and happy; and the companion of her childhood and youth had never become an object of envy, nor ever ceased to be a sister. Meanwhile, the God of providence would have provided well for Leah; and He who, when she was neglected by her husband, "looked upon her affliction," would have led her to a better happiness than that to which she was clandestinely conducted, on the sad night of Jacob's deception.

Well, peace to the memory of Leah, the less beloved! The shadows of melancholy that gather over her history are yet strongly tinged with beauty. The sympathies of a hundred generations linger around her name. More truly than of any other one, may be it be said of her, that she was "a mother in Israel." None with a purer and louder song gave praise unto God. One-half of "the twelve patriarchs" were born of her; while from one of her sons, as concerning the flesh, the Messiah came, who is over all, God blessed forever. When, on the last day of time, the trump of God shall agitate the sacred dust of Machpelah, the form of Leah shall be seen rising in glory, side by side with those of Abraham, Isaac, and Jacob; and in the arrangements of Heaven, she shall take her place among the "daughters who have done virtuously."

Nor must we wrong Rachel, the beloved and beautiful. She evinced, it is true, that she was not an angel of light. There were faults—decided faults, in her character; and who of her sex would not have betrayed some of them, if placed in similar relations? Did she not know, that *for her* it was that her husband toiled through those seven years, which seemed so brief for the love he bore her? Did she not know that Jacob sought for her, and for no other; that he had designed no other companion of his life? And was it then so strange, that she should count her own a prior and a stronger claim to him who had preferred her? Thus, had she not even aggravated inducements to dissatisfaction, jealousy, and envy? Let us, then, accord to her the benefit of such palliations. Let us remember her as human, and, therefore, more or less imperfect. At the same time, we will contemplate her as the beloved of Jacob, and as one who was heard and honored of God. Let us rejoice in her joy, as she became the mother of the illustrious Joseph. Let us weep for her grief, as, at the birth of Benjamin, she exclaimed, in dying, "Child of my sorrow!" "Child of my right hand!" responded the heart-broken father, as he loved him then, and always—loved him most tenderly, for the sake of her that bare him. Let us note where she died, and lies buried; the spot of all the earth which she might select where to lay aside her mortal vestments—where Christ, the promised Seed, should first appear, and within hearing of the accompanying hosannas from eternity—the first and last song from angel voices, falling on the ears of mortal men. There Jacob left the faded form of his beloved Rachel—the tear of her last sorrow still moistening her brow, as he laid her away in the chambers of darkness. Long afterwards—and when the infants of Bethlehem were bleeding and dying—the voice of inspiration, with matchless felicity, and in the poetry of heaven, sung of her as rousing from her long sleep, to listen to the mournful tragedy, and weeping yet again!—weeping for her slaughtered children, and refusing to be comforted!

Rachel! When He shall come the second time, to gather all his chosen ones, and wipe away their tears forever, thou shalt be there!

Pharaoh's Daughter.

Pharaoh's daughter will always be an object of interest among the female characters of the Holy Scriptures. The great Jewish historian, and the Jewish Targums and doctors, generally assign to her the name of *Thermuthis*. She was the daughter of that stupid and wicked prince then reigning in Egypt, who, in order to the depression and utter subjugation of the enslaved Israelites, imposed the additional burdens upon that unfortunate people, and issued orders for the murder, at their birth, of all their male children. Let us discern here, in passing, one of those singular providences, by which God often causes wicked men to fight against themselves, and, while they imagine they are dealing utter destruction upon others, are only driving the blade of ruin deeply and fatally into their own vitals. Pharaoh orders the destruction of the male infants. The infant of Jochebed is consequently exposed in the ark of bulrushes. The daughter of the murderer himself discovers the child. He thus becomes her adopted son, and receives an education suited to an Egyptian prince, and becomes specially qualified to act, in the sequel, as God's agent in the utter overthrow of the power that sought to destroy him and his nation. When will men learn the absurdity of unrighteousness! Pharaoh may contrive and counsel; yet God has him in hand all the while, and will make him a mere illustration of the Divine power and skill, that will cause every blow of the tyrant to come down upon his own pate, and lay him prostrate at last, amid the crushings of remediless ruin.

What was the character of Pharaoh's daughter, we are not permitted to know with definiteness. That she partook, more or less, of the diabolical disposition of her father, we are not informed, and need not infer. It is pleasant to perceive that no evil thing is recorded of her. If she had faults, the pen of inspiration has kindly spared them; while most that is written, exhibits her under aspects such as any princess of this world might covet. There are innocence and beauty in all the part she plays in the early history of Israel's great lawgiver. We follow her with deep interest, as, in company with her maidens, she roams, that day, along the banks of the Nile. We watch her, as her attention becomes arrested by the unusual object among the reeds at the river's brink. We almost hear her voice, as she gives directions to one of her attendants to bring it up upon the bank. We mark her graceful movements, as she cautiously lays open the secret treasure—and partake of her interest as, with sudden astonishment, she looks down upon that sobbing, yet beautiful boy. We love her for the gushing compassion of her heart, as she gazed upon that exposed, and homeless, and cheerless infant,—and for the kiss of affection which, doubtless, touched that moment the lips of the weeping. We love her the more deeply, as we hear her exclaim, "Of the Hebrews' children this!" He is one of those innocent, yet proscribed babes, doomed, by her father, to yield up the breath they have just received. But goodness and pity still linger within the halls of the murderous Pharaoh; and where there are blood, and shrieks, and dying cries, may be heard, swelling above the murmurings of despair, one voice so beautiful as though a seraph whispered. A sister's watchful eyes, as was meet, were upon the scene of the discovery. "Shall I run for a nurse from the Hebrews?" she asks of the noble princess. "Run!" responds that sprightly and compassionate voice; while, as the nurse and mother comes, it adds, "Take this boy away, and nurse him for me." Thus, there is life instead of death,—and great joy, rather than the mourning and weeping which will not be comforted.

A fairer day than that never before arose over the daughter of Pharaoh. A finer sport had never awaited her, amid her rambles and rejoicings by that noble stream. Never before had she so triumphantly played the part of angels, as sung, long afterward, by the "sweet psalmist of Israel." An unseen Hand was near her—giving her charge over the future "man of God," to keep him in all his ways—drawing him out of many waters—bearing him up in her hands—and bringing him forth into a large place. And if the infant Moses was a type of the infant Jesus—and if the murdered innocents of Egypt foreshadowed those at Bethlehem—and if the bloody Herod answered back to hateful Pharaoh, as deep calleth unto deep—then what beauteous being, whispering amid the dreams of Mary's husband, echoed the voice of her who, in the ears of Moses's mother, uttered, "Take this child away!"

And the child was taken away—taken from death, like the virgin's babe—and grew and flourished till he came again into the presence of his illustrious protectress, and became the son of her adoption. She it was who gave to him the name so greatly distinguished on earth, and has long since been written in the book of life; and will be often named with holy admiration among the circles of immortality. Nor was she neglectful of the interesting charge which she had undertaken. As she commenced in good faith, so she continued the steadfast friend—the kind benefactress—the munificent and devoted mother. She withheld no privileges of mental or physical discipline—no books or tutors—nor any means available to the Egyptian court, for his education and greatness. Nor were her attentions and efforts unsuccessful; for her son became learned in all the wisdom of the Egyptians, and mighty in words and deeds.

Nor am I able to discern, with some, so abundant reproach upon the patroness of Moses, springing from the fact of his declining, on coming to age, the honor which she had generously proffered him—the honor of being her own son, and inheriting all the privileges incident to such a distinguished relation. By that faith, of which he was one of the bright examples, he chose to identify himself with his own people and the people of God; and that, too, notwithstanding all their deep afflictions. To become an Egyptian, and an Egyptian prince, with a prospect even of the throne of Pharaoh—might be highly conducive to his happiness as a worldly man; but a greater prize was in his eye, and he aspired after the rewards of eternity.

All this speaks nothing very severe against her who, next to his own parents, had been his best earthly friend. It only tells of his resigning his earthly prospects, which were of a most auspicious character, that he might secure the better and more enduring substance. How this decision of Moses affected her who had befriended him—or whether she survived to witness such a step on his part, the record is silent. Utter darkness here settles down upon the history of this distinguished princess. For a brief space she appears upon the stage—assumes a part of surpassing interest—performs with exceeding propriety and dignity—gives utterance to music that charms the world, and whose echoings will "wander through eternity,"—then retires suddenly and forever. A vision of awful judgments soon succeeds; there are lightnings, and tempests, and bloody spectres, and dashing floods; yet "Pharaoh's daughter" is away, and there is no light!—none save the glimmerings reflected from a life whose visible points were only beautiful. There is somewhere living a suspicion, that the early friend and benefactress of Moses never witnessed the dread disasters which, through his awful mediation, swept, in after time, over her devoted country. Who shall say that she was not taken away from the evil to come? And, lingering in my thoughts, with the fullness of her native pity and generosity—with the fact that she was the providential agent of preserving, rearing, and educating a great "prince in Israel,"—and the possible and probable influence exerted upon her mind and heart by the example of the son of her adoption,—and *such* a son,—who shall forbid me from gathering up, though tremblingly, the welcome conclusion that, if not before, yet when the death-shades drew over her, like the darkness where the infant Moses was cradled, one of the Beatitudes of eternal goodness came where she lay,—broke in upon her darkness, and sung in the ear of her departing spirit, "Blessed are the merciful, for they shall obtain mercy."

Miriam.

It would be wrong to omit Miriam in these brief notices of the women of the Bible. We cannot help regarding her with reverence, not only as being the sister of the great Moses, but the first prophetess of whom we have any record. She could not have been less than ten years the senior of Moses, inasmuch as she was, doubtless, the sister that watched him when exposed in the ark of bulrushes, and aided so materially in carrying out the stratagem for his preservation. After this, we hear no more of Miriam until just after the Exodus, and amid the festivities and rejoicings consequent upon the escape of the Israelites, and the destruction of their enemies and pursuers in the Red Sea. At this time she must have been, at least, ninety years of age; and, of course, was venerable for years, as well as for the position she held, as associated with her two brethren in the leadership of Israel. That such was her official relation, seems hinted by the scenery of the rejoicings already alluded to. For while Moses led the great chorus of the sons of Israel, in the song of triumph over Pharaoh,—Miriam, on the other hand, at the head of all the women, with timbrels and dances, answered back the glad notes of praise unto God. And while the Psalmist presents the people of God as led, like a flock, by the hand of Moses and Aaron—regarding them as the principal leaders—the prophet Micah adds Miriam, by name, to her two brothers, as being associated with them in this great commission. We may recognize an entire fitness in such an arrangement, and especially as connected with Eastern customs, relative to the separation of the two sexes in their assemblies, joined, also, in the case of the Israelites, with their itinerating position. As a prophetess, she doubtless instructed the female portion of the community, as her brothers instructed their own sex,—while the record of the difficulty at Hazeroth seems to afford additional proof of their joint, though not equal, participation in leading and teaching the people.

From this view, it seems fair to assign to Miriam a very elevated place among the women whose names appear upon the inspired page. An elder and only sister of two of the most distinguished and honored of all men—herself partaking with them of the prophetic illumination—and bearing so important a part as leader of the women of Israel, not only in their songs and rejoicings, but also as a divinely-appointed instructress—she deserves a place in our thoughts, in sacred association with her illustrious brothers. If we assign to Moses the mediatorship of the great legal dispensation,—and to Aaron the first place in the Levitical priesthood,—so also to Miriam we are to accord the honor of being the earliest of the recorded prophetesses, as well as the most distinguished of all the daughters that danced in triumph over the spoiling of their Egyptian foes.

Yet a shade appears upon the fair fame of Miriam. She evinces to us that, with all her advantages and dignity, she is but human, and subject to human frailties.

In common with her brother Aaron, she appears not to have fancied the wife of Moses—her whom he had married in Midian, and whom he had returned, for a season, to her father, previously to the judgments that fell upon Egypt. During the stay of the Israelites in the vicinity of Sinai, Zipporah returned to her husband, accompanied by her father and her two sons. This was, probably, the first interview between the sister and wife of Moses, and shortly after arose the difficulty, whose results were so alarming, and so disreputable to Miriam. We are taught that she, in connection with Aaron, found fault with Moses by reason of his alliance with a woman of another nation, while their displeasure on this account very naturally associated itself with envy at his pre-eminence as a prophet of God. This displeasure and envy broke forth into bitter words and dark questionings between Miriam and Aaron, touching their brother. Lord, what is man—or what is woman! Had they not seen the great distinction which God had so obviously given to their brother? Had they forgotten the awful judgments of Egypt, and the part he acted in those frightful manifestations? Had not the thunders of Sinai just ceased—voices so terrible, that those who heard them entreated that they might hear them no more? Was not the pillar of cloud and fire suspended with unearthly sublimity over the encampment? Needed they to be reminded that Moses was the appointed agent in these great movements, and the presiding genius amid this strange scenery? Must those great and distinguished personages suddenly receive a public and terrible admonition? Must God come down —and Aaron and Miriam be called forth, and instructed by special communication, as to the position of their brother, and his universal faithfulness—and reminded that he was the one, such as there was no other; to whom the Lord spake face to face, and mouth to mouth? With amazing emphasis, therefore, must the question have come home: "Why, then, were ye not afraid to speak against my servant Moses?" And there was the kindling of God's anger—and his departure—and the uplifting of the cloud from the tabernacle; and lo! the great prophetess—the most eminent of her sex through all that assembled nation—Miriam—poor Miriam, was a leper! "Heal her now, I beseech thee," cried the injured brother; and his was a prayer that almost always was greatly availing with God. She was healed, though doomed to a temporary exclusion from the camp; and seven days all Israel waited for Miriam amid the wilds of Hazeroth.

Let him that thinketh he standeth, take heed

lest he fall! Amid exaltation or depression—prosperity or adversity—how wise, how necessary to guard our spirit, and set a watch upon the door of our lips, lest, in an evil hour, Satan shall gain an advantage over us. The blemish of Miriam should instruct every one—her own sex especially—to speak advisedly—to repress the earliest risings of vanity or impure ambition—to look well—each one—to her own ways; and, in a quiet and contented spirit, fulfill, with dignity and pleasure, the appropriate duties of her own sphere of action. Providence and revelation both have assigned their respective places to man and to woman, and all attempts at interference, the one with the other's special province of action, will infallibly insure the contempt of all enlightened spectators, and the displeasure of Him who rules that every one move "in his own order."

After the events above referred to, we hear little of Miriam. She survived to the great age of, at least, one hundred and thirty years; and when the congregation of Israel, after long wanderings, came to Kadesh, there they buried, presently, the distinguished and only sister of Moses and Aaron. Her aged brothers followed her in haste. Aaron slept on Mount Hor, about four months after the death of Miriam at Kadesh;—and just *twelve* months after her death, the nation of Israel were passing over Jordan,—and Moses, of course, was absent! From the heights of Pisgah he had seen the pledged inheritance stretching far away to "the utmost sea." Afterwards the great Moses died, and his funeral was singular and awful—God buried him;—and his tomb is—somewhere!

Thus, within one brief year, died those illustrious three. So passes the glory of the world. And in *such* a year! Those tedious wanderings, and wearisome sojournings, that consumed so many of their precious days, were almost finished. Mysterious and awful providences had walked, like the footsteps of God, amid their latter years. Might not the clouds at last retire—and the thunderings die away—and, reposing their weary forms upon some green spot over amid those promised fields, might they not be permitted to see their sun sink cloudlessly to its setting—and with their trembling feet to tread, if but once, the land promised to the ancient three, and where they lay buried?

Hush, every murmur! He doeth all things well. Weep not for the hour when the aged righteous pass away to heaven.

> "Farewell, conflicting hopes and fears,
> Where lights and shades alternate dwell;
> How bright the unchanging morn appears!
> Farewell, inconstant world, farewell!"

Zipporah.

WE would fain give a passing tribute to her who was wife of the great Moses. But few words are said of her in the sacred record; and the holy man, who was commissioned to write of others, seems to have been directed to pen but a line or two of the companion of his life, and the mother of his children.

The history of Moses' marriage bears a striking resemblance to that of his great ancestor, Jacob. As at forty years of age the latter was compelled to flee for his life from his native country, so Moses also, at the same age, and for the same object. As the one, in his pilgrimage, found, after long wanderings, a shepherdess, and helped to water her flock, and received the hospitalities of her father's house—so did the other. As, in the one instance, the fair shepherdess became the wife of the stranger, so in the other. And as, in the case of the more ancient pair, the good providence of God may have seemed to design the meeting and the alliance, may we not suppose that the same wise direction was concerned in the union of Moses and the Ethiopian maid? This great man, possessed of extensive learning and rare capacities—and a prince in the matter of his education and accomplishments, was not the one to contract a hasty and injudicious alliance; and it may be safely inferred, that the woman of his choice was more than ordinary in respect to her character and abilities. It will not be forgotten that she was the daughter of no ordinary man—one who was capable, by his great wisdom, of advising and instructing his son-in-law concerning the government of the Israelites, and whose instructions were respected and followed, to the great relief and benefit, both of Moses and the numerous people under his charge. Nor will it be forgotten that this same man, so much respected by Moses, was a man of God. Being a descendant of Abraham by Keturah, he retained the knowledge of the true God, so specially and abundantly given to his illustrious ancestor; and knew how, at once, on hearing of the Divine goodness to his son-in-law and the Israelites, to bless the Lord who had delivered them from the Egyptians—while, in his character of priest, he offered up burnt-offerings and sacrifices in praise of Him whom he knew to be greater than all gods.

Regarding, therefore, on the one hand, the character and capacity of her venerable father,—and those, on the other hand, of the man who selected her as his companion and wife—we may, amid the silence of inspiration on the subject, infer for Zipporah an elevated place among women. And if but little is said or hinted of her excellences on the holy page, who shall say but the very fact of her relation to him who, by the Holy Ghost, was moved to write that page, may, in part, if not in whole, explain the omission? We have seen her in her youth a shepherdess, with her sisters, superintending their father's flock. On the arrival of Moses from Egypt, she, with the approbation of her father, became the wife of the exile, and the mother of two sons. When her husband received the Divine commission to return to Egypt, she, together with her children, accompanied him. The extraordinary incident related of their journey has been thought to reflect, more or less, upon the character of Zipporah. Yet our judgment should be kind touching a matter that is confessedly mysterious. Moses, a circumcised Israelite, would naturally desire to distinguish, by the rite of his nation, his own sons. His wife was of another family and nation, where the same rite was probably not observed. Under these circumstances, there might easily arise a strong objection to the bloody ceremony, as performed upon her children. To her influence the meek and gentle Moses may be supposed to have yielded, until God met him, and convinced him that further delay would be fatal. And when, under these stringent circumstances, she at last yielded, it may have been—it *seems* to have been—with an accompanying reproach against her husband, while an unbecoming gesture attended an unbecoming reflection upon his character as a husband and a man of goodness.

Whether it was from the above-named incident,

or in view of the solemn mission which, in connection with his brother, he was about to fulfill in Egypt; or whether it was from some other cause, that Moses directed Zipporah's temporary return, with their sons, to Midian, seems not to be well understood. She returned to her father, and remained with him during the dreadful judgments upon Pharaoh and his people—and until the arrival of her husband and the Israelites in the vicinity of Mount Sinai. Her father then accompanied her and her sons, as she came to join her husband in the wilderness, and to identify herself and her children with the fortunes of Moses and the nation of Israel. The meeting of Moses and Jethro, and the mutual greetings, communications, and rejoicings that followed, amply testify the pleasure of both parties on the occasion, and speak much for the mutual esteem and affection between the man of God and his beloved family.

And if such was the state of affairs, then should all parties have been satisfied; and he who was laden down with the multiplied cares of his most arduous station, ought to have been left unmolested to partake of the consolations thus providentially proffered him, in the return and presence of his domestic circle. Not so thought Miriam and Aaron. They had previously only heard of their brother's wife; but now, upon her arrival in the camp—a stranger from another country than theirs—they complain of Moses because of "the

Ethiopian woman" whom he had seen fit to wed. Alas for us, when we venture a reproach against him whom the Lord loves and approves! Whosoever touches such a one, touches the apple of God's eye. Such was the hapless position of her who should have shown herself the sister, rather than the reprover, of Moses and his wife; and thus did she incur the condemnation of those who take up a reproach against the innocent.

Here closes the scene. He who wrote of the death and burial of Sarah, Rebecca, and Rachel, was restrained from recording the sickness and decease of his beloved Zipporah;—while of her sepulchre may it be said, as truly as of that of her illustrious husband, "no man knoweth where it is until this day."

Jephthah's Daughter.

Two months of her history comprise all that we certainly know of the daughter of Jephthah. She is first introduced to us when grown up to youth, and as being the only child of her father. What remains of the account is in connection with the rash vow of her parent,—of which the disastrous influence fell with all its weight upon his beautiful and unfortunate child.

Jephthah, leading the host of Israel against the Ammonites, made a vow to the Lord, of which the following is the authorized translation:—

"If thou shalt, without fail, deliver the children of Ammon into my hands, then it shall be that whatsoever cometh forth of the doors of my house to meet me when I return in peace from the children of Ammon, shall surely be the Lord's; and I will offer it up for a burnt-offering."

We can hardly wonder that many, and even some learned commentators, understood from this vow, and the sequel, that the daughter of Jephthah, who happened to be the one that "came forth of the doors" to meet her father on his return, was actually slain by him after the manner of burnt-offerings. It is pleasant, however, to meditate, that there are strong, if not irresistible, reasons against such a melancholy view. These reasons may be summed up as follows:

Every scholar knows that the Hebrew *copulative* is often *disjunctive* also;—especially in case of repetition, as here. Hence, the true reading may be, and doubtless is, "Whatever cometh forth of the doors of my house—either shall be the Lord's, or I will offer it up for a burnt-offering."

The sacrifice of children to Moloch was ever an abomination to the Lord. Of course such a sacrifice *to the Lord* must have been a still greater abomination in his sight,—an abomination for which there is no precedent or example. The sacrifice of Isaac was never actually made, nor was it ever intended on the part of God.

No father had power to put his child to death,

as obvious from Deut. xxi, 18–21. King Saul himself was forcibly restrained from slaughtering his son Jonathan, in fulfillment of a vow which he had made.

To kill an innocent person was directly forbidden by the law of God;—and, on the hypothesis that Jephthah was a righteous man, he would not deliberately commit a great crime, for the sake of fulfilling a rash and unjustifiable vow.

Two entire months elapsed after his return, before he fulfilled his vow. Of course, there was ample time for consideration and a correct decision, even had he, at first, designed the death of his daughter.

The vow, and the intended fulfillment, together with the time, were all public; nor is it rational to suppose that so revolting a tragedy as the destruction of his only child would be tolerated by the people. There was the fullest opportunity for interference, and such interference would have actually taken place, as not long afterward for the rescue of Jonathan.

These considerations appear sufficiently conclusive, that Jephthah never shed the blood of his daughter;—while the sequel of the story seems entirely confirmatory of this view. At the end of two months, she returned from her wanderings in the mountains of Gilead, to afford her father an opportunity for the fulfillment of his vow; "and he did with her according to his vow." That is, she became the Lord's, and consecrated to him, like the thirty-two virgins which were the Lord's portion of the Midianitish captives, and who aided to keep charge of the tabernacle of the Lord. Num. xxxi, 31–41.

Eminent beauty is apparent in the character of Jephthah's daughter. We are delighted with her first appearance. Her victorious father has arrived in the vicinity, having subdued the enemies of his country, and is come to Mizpeh, where is the seat of his residence. Of course, there are great rejoicings. Thousands are abroad to greet the "mighty man of valor" as he approaches. Meanwhile, there is *one* whose soul swells in rapturous sympathy with the festivities of that day. Yet she is not overcome by the excitement. There is no ungraceful haste or exposure. With delightful modesty, propriety, and dignity, she tarries for her father in her father's house,—tarries till he comes. Then, as was meet, she makes her appearance. She has waited till the exact moment, concealed, as we would prefer, from the confused crowd. Nor yet has she waited in idleness or indifference. A select company of her associates are there, and all are arranged in becoming dress, and their instruments of music are in their hands. The father appears, and the daughter comes out to meet him with timbrels and dances. Thus, long before, did Miriam and the women of Israel, when the "horse and his rider were thrown into the sea." Thus, long afterwards, was the victorious David greeted, as from many a city, with singing and dancing, and instruments of music, the daughters of Israel chanted in his ear their joyous salutations.

But here ends, alas! the gladness and glory of the festival of Mizpeh. The sprightly notes of the timbrel, and the brilliant voices of the maidens of Gilead, and the shouts of the gathered crowds—all suddenly die away on the ear; and there is deep lamentation, and rending of garments—and the mighty man is brought low—very low; and the beautiful child—the only one—becomes "one of his troubles"—the innocent occasion of sore and boundless grief. "Alas, my daughter!" ay; and alas for ten thousand delicious hopes of this strange world! The greatest joy, they say, may all suddenly become transmuted to the deepest sorrow; and within the sweetest rose of the vale may be concealed a sting, the agony of whose piercings may long survive the deceitful blossom we venture carelessly to touch. How striking the lesson of this day to the triumphant Jephthah! How has a mysterious Providence bowed him to the dust! After this, will he ever again confide in terrestrial hopes? In the midst of prosperity, and joyful conquest, and personal elevation, will he not walk softly—and cease to trust in a human arm—and lean upon the Strong alone?

But our sympathies linger not with the father alone. We think of her on whom the sad reverses of this day fall most fatally. We look with intensest interest to see what will be her bearing, as she passes beneath the mournful cloud. We listen to catch the words she will utter, as the darkness is already enshrouding her. As we wait, music, more beautiful by far than the notes of the timbrel, swells amid the gloom. "My father! thou hast opened thy mouth to Jehovah—do to me accordingly, since thine enemies are conquered." Here we behold the child of deep and sweet simplicity. Here breathes the spirit of holy and sublime piety;—the great God is recognized. There must be no lightness in his presence—all vows and promises to him must be remembered, whatever be the present sorrows they involve. Let him be honored, though our poor name be heard no longer among the thousands of Israel. Here glow the charms of filial obedience. There is no rebellion—no resistance—no displeasure—no murmur. The response of those lips breathed but the soft notes of submission and cheerful acquiescence. Here—even in the midst of the fires—swells the voice of heavenly gratitude. "Pay thy vows, my father; for the Lord hath avenged thee of thy enemies! Let my worldly prospects be sacrificed, if such a sacrifice shall praise Him who hath helped us."

After the two months upon the mountains of Gilead, the child of Jephthah returned to her father, who "did with her according to his vow." She was not a "mother in Israel;" but she was one of Israel's fairest, loveliest daughters. If, in her life, she walked solitary—and lover and friend were put far from her—and joyous children arose not up to call her blessed,—yet did the Lord take her up, and revealed her beauty to the eyes of all after generations, who will forever count her among the daughters that are "as corner-stones—polished after the similitude of a palace."

Deborah and Jael.

Deborah was a prophetess, and one of the line of Judges that presided over the people, from the days of Joshua and the elders that survived him, to the establishment of the regal government under Saul. She was wife of Lapidoth, and her residence was beneath a palm-tree on Mount Ephraim, a few miles northerly from Jerusalem, whither the people of Israel resorted for judgment. In her time the Israelites were under bondage to Jabin, a powerful king of northern Canaan, who, for twenty years, was permitted, by a judicial Providence, to oppress them, on account of their idolatry and general wickedness. The time had come, however, for their deliverance ; and Deborah commanded Barak, her chief captain—then residing in the north—to summon from Zebulon and Naphtali,—the two tribes nearest in vicinity to the tyrant, Jabin,—a force of ten thousand men, and attack Sisera, his general ;—assuring him, by prophecy, of success and victory. The two armies met near the river Kishon, the forces of Sisera were completely routed, he himself, abandoning his chariot, fled on foot for his life. His course lay toward the dominions of Jabin, and arriving in the vicinity of Kadesh, he is met by Jael, wife of Heber, who was professedly friendly to Jabin. She forthwith invites the fugitive general into her tent—still professes friendship and peace—and proffers hospitality and concealment from his pursuers. Through excessive weariness, after his long flight and great excitement, he presently falls asleep; when Jael, providing herself with a long tent-nail, or spike, with a mallet smites it through his temples, and pins him to the earth—a murdered man. Thus the oppression of Jabin over Israel was broken, and the land had rest from its enemies during forty years.

Deborah was present with her general and army on the decisive day above noticed;—and her name is famous principally, perhaps, from the song she composed and sung in connection with Barak, on occasion of her brilliant victory over the king of Canaan. This song is highly distinguished for sublimity and beauty, and takes rank with the highest style of poetry. It commences, as is meet, with praise to Jehovah, and ascribes to him all the prosperity of Israel, from their earliest deliverances down to the present triumph. The names of most of Israel's ranks are caught up in its sublime sweep, as it breathes reproach upon one, and praise upon another, according as they severally lingered at their homes, or rallied against the mighty foe of their common country. The lofty muse of Deborah contemplates even the stars of heaven themselves as marshaling their shining ranks against the enemies of Israel, and the river of Kishon as being maddened into fury, and sweeping them away with swift destruction.

But why, one may ask, breathes this song a blessing upon the murderer of Sisera? Her husband's house is at profound peace with Jabin. Sisera, in his flight from his conquerors, solicits refuge with Jael, as being not unfriendly to his master's cause. She meets him beyond her doors —invites him to her tent—quiets his fears—provides a place of concealment—and ministers to his wants. Sisera, in his excessive weariness, presently sleeps, and in that slumber is killed by his pretended benefactress. What is this but murder—aggravated murder—compassed by heartless, cruel treachery? The character and deserts of Sisera are here out of the question. It may be easy to admit, that his measure of iniquity was full, and that his death, with all the baseness and cruelty of the accompanying circumstances, was justly due;—yet there is no exculpation of Jael. We must write her a murderess, and such, we think, must be the verdict of every enlightened conscience. No one loves the name and memory of Jael. We think of her as a bloody woman. "Her mouth is smoother than oil, but her end is bitter as wormwood—sharp as a two-edged sword." Her tent is stained with blood. The noise of slaughter and the shrieks of the dying are there. The winds of heaven moan as they breathe along the plains of Zaanaim. No inviting scenery allures the footstep. Beauty and innocence are absent—deceit, treachery, cruelty, laugh there, and the blows of the assassin are the music of the hateful sport.

What, then, of the blessing? Is it from the Lord? There is a CURSE from him upon the one who does evil that good may come. Deceit and falsehood are ever an abomination in his sight. Then he had no approval for the shameless, heartless Jael, nor does Deborah bless her from the Lord. No blessing falls to her as being good and righteous,—but as having uncommon courage rather,—as having a firmness of nerve sufficient to "put her hand to the nail, and her right hand to the workman's hammer," and smite. Such a species of daring was hers in an eminent degree, and "above women" in general. For this she is praised, and for nothing else; and a similar commendation has been often appropriately given to characters who, like Jael, were among the deformed and graceless of the world.

Delilah.

UNHAPPY name! Will her sex pardon me, that I am obliged to write it among others that are so fragrant and pure? Here all is shadow. There appears no redeeming feature. It is true, we may suspect her to have been attractive in person, for a strong man bowed before her. But what is a comely exterior, where it covers naught save deformity? What of the glowing colors of the poisonous serpent? Or what the variegated brilliancy of the hateful leopard? The heavenly pen sketched nothing good of Delilah. She was "a woman in the valley of Sorek." No ancestor or child of hers is named—her nation is unknown—her "valley," no one can point it out. "His roots shall be dried up beneath, and above shall his branch be cut off;—his remembrance shall perish from the earth, and he shall have no name in the street."

Delilah was a shameless seducer. "And a man void of understanding, passing through the street near her corner, went the way to her house in the twilight—in the evening—in the black and dark night; and there met him a woman, and with her much fair speech she caused him to yield—with the flattering of her lips she forced him. He goeth after her straightway as an ox goeth to the slaughter, or as a fool to the correction of the stocks, till a dart strike through his liver,—as a bird hasteth to the snare, and knoweth not that it is for his life."

She was a heartless deceiver. Feigning affection for her lover, she, with unyielding pertinacity, sought his desolation and ruin. Her mouth was smoother than oil, but her end bitter as wormwood—sharp as a two-edged sword. The deceived one—strangers were filled with his wealth, and his labors were in the house of a stranger, and he mourned at the last.

She was disgustingly covetous. For money, she could readily dispense with every principle of righteousness or honor. Her own emolument and aggrandizement were instead of all goodness, purity, and love. "Entice him, and we will give thee silver," was a note sufficient for her ear, and to induce her, like the faithless reptile, to sting the bosom that cherished her.

She was a foul traitress. She, like a certain other, betrayed with a kiss. She fondled the victim she designed to immolate. Her eyes were as full of murder as of adultery. Like a certain horrid idol of heathenism, she pretended to embrace most affectionately, yet, as her arms enfolded the hapless object, he was pierced by a hundred concealed and deadly blades. She cast down the wounded—a strong man was slain by her. Her house was the way to hell, going down to the chambers of death.

Such was Delilah, the infamous. Furnished

she not a portion of the materials, when the wise man drew his picture of "The Strange Woman?"

Let us weep for the frightfulness of the serpent. Sin, alas, how mournful and sickening is its aspect! With what horror we contemplate the near approach to which it advances us toward the character of the utterly wicked and lost! O! how it has defaced and spoiled the fair image of angelic goodness and beauty! Be there eternal praises to Him whose "grace much more abounds!"

Naomi.

We emerge again, suddenly, into fairer regions, where, away from scenes of darkness and deceit—of impurity and death, more graceful forms come forth to greet us, and lovelier airs breathe over the landscape, and heavenly Virtue, as the presiding genius, waves her golden sceptre.

Naomi was the wife of Elimelech, a citizen of Bethlehem, and who lived in the time of the Judges. There being a famine in Judea, he, with his family, consisting of his wife, Naomi, and their two sons, emigrated to the country of Moab. Elimelech died shortly after his removal; and within about ten years, the sons, who had married in Moab, both of them also died. Thus Naomi the mother, and the two daughters-in-law, named Orpah and Ruth, became widows. Under these melancholy circumstances, Naomi, having learned that abundance had succeeded to famine in her native country, determined to return thither, and spend her remaining days with her kindred. The family commenced the journey accordingly. Before proceeding far, however, Naomi, addressing her daughters-in-law, very affectingly advised, and even entreated them both to return to their former homes—explaining to them, in the most faithful manner, how discouraging were their prospects by remaining with her, and accompanying her to a foreign land. Orpah—though with great reluctance and with many tears—gave to her mother the kiss of adieu, and returned home. Ruth, however, could not be persuaded to leave her widowed and aged relative, and attended her to Bethlehem, where a peaceful evening closed up the stormy day of life that had passed over the bereaved and desolate Naomi.

The history impresses us with deep and affecting interest. Viewing her, as her husband and sons are buried, and herself alone in that distant and gentile land, there rises a fit picture for all bereaved spirits to contemplate. And let them recall to mind, meanwhile, that their own is not the first, and probably not the deepest sorrow that has struck and broken the human heart. How true to nature are the sighings of this lone widow to tread, once more, her native soil! The dearest objects of her love are removed from her sight;—she would fain go home, that she may die with their kindred and hers. Though the record is silent here, yet is it too much to imagine, that ere she "went forth out of the place where she was," she lingered long and sadly over those three graves; and as she remembered other and happier years, and forms that were beauty and glory to her eye, she knew, in that dark hour, all the bitterness of grief? Tearing herself away at last, and turning her face toward her fatherland, and journeying wearily and heavily, and pondering—as she went—her present desolation, and all the hopelessness shadowing the future—she pauses in the way; and now opens a scene which, in mournful tenderness—in deep and touching pathos, has been surpassed by few that have ever appealed to human sympathies. Why should she involve others in her own hard and cheerless destiny? Since joy might yet remain to her daughters, though none to her, why should she wish their desolation to be added to hers, and lead them away from their kindred, to die with her in widowhood and tears? Here generosity and grief become beautifully blended. Here rises a spectacle of profoundest sorrow, accompanied, however, with the coolest and tenderest consideration. Desolate grief, and prudent and disinterested counsel, here form a union as charming to contemplation, as it is honorable to humanity. "Go," said Naomi to her daughters, "return each to her mother's house; and the Lord deal kindly with you, as ye have dealt with the dead and with me!" She submits—nay, desires to be left alone. Her only friends in that strange land are permitted to go their own way. She would mourn apart. A mother's house, with its varied consolations, is theirs; but father and mother have forsaken her, and lover and friend are hidden from her. The widowed three have been as one hitherto,—their interests,—their toils and sorrows were blended. The mother asks now that the union, though affectionate and cordial, shall be dissolved, and their destinies be henceforth separate. She would be left with the dead—and begs the young to return to the living, and forget the alliance which, though pleasant when in being, yet now has passed forever away. "Deal kindly with you, as you—with the dead and with me!" Interests two—separate—divided! Alas, what was the pang of that bitter moment, as it rent to utter bleeding that poor widow's heart! Will she bear up to add yet another prayer? "The Lord grant you to find rest, each in her husband's house!" For them new alliances and brighter days were probable, wherein the griefs of the past would rise on the eye as distant and flitting shadows, while soft and cheering sunshine should play around the present. Not so with her. No "husband's house" awaited her more. For her no green spot arose in prospect—there would be no smile to light on her—no arm would be reached forth to her in her weariness, and when she should "find rest," it would be that of the tomb. As she prints the farewell kiss, "We will return with thee!" respond the weeping children. "Turn again, my daughters! Why will ye go with me? With me all is desolation—there are no more husbands—no more pleasant homes. As the fig-tree alone in the desert, scathed of the lightning, and withered and fruitless—so is your sorrowful mother. It grieveth me much, for your sakes, that the hand of the Lord hath gone out against me." Again the voice of bitter weeping bursts upon the ear—the parting kiss of Orpah is given, and the next moment she disappears forever. "Return after thy sister!" The command is vain. Another destiny awaits the devoted Ruth, and the younger and the more aged widow pass, hand in hand, toward Judea.

One day, there is an unusual excitement in Bethlehem. Two lonely women, arriving from another country, in weariness and sadness, enter the quiet city. The name of *Naomi* is whispered from house to house, and rumors and inquiries pass rapidly from circle to circle. It is long since, with her husband, strong in his ripened manhood, and her sons, sprightly in youthful vigor and hope, she sought a distant and gentile home. Since then, there is no intelligence. Have they, at last, returned? "Is this Naomi?" She treads the sacred dust where beloved forms once moved in beauty, but are now passed away. Perchance she seeks the very mansion, and reclines mournfully in those same apartments where her departed husband was wont to "bless his house," and whence, in happier years, the morning and evening orisons went up to heaven. As she looks, and meditates, and remembers—the wormwood and the gall are renewed—again is the great deep broken up, and the fountains are opened—and the billows pass over the bereaved. "Call me not Naomi! Call me Mara! for very bitterly hath the Almighty dealt with me. I went out full, and he hath returned me empty."

Yet a peaceful evening awaits the sorrowful Naomi after the storms that, in mournful repetition, were suffered to beat upon her fragile form. There is One that sitteth on high, who rules the tempest. "Call upon me in the day of trouble," he saith, "I will deliver thee!" She sought rest for her daughter, and He who "is able to give abundantly more than we ask," while he provided rest and joy for the child, gave quietness and abundance to the mother.

Somewhere in Bethlehem stood a princely residence, where dwelt "a mighty man of wealth,"—and good and noble, as he was rich and powerful. Great festivities were shortly witnessed within that mansion, and smiling groups might have been seen there presenting their congratulations to Naomi, at her resting-place in the house of Boaz, the husband of Ruth the Beautiful.

The moral of this tale appeals to the heart of the widow. Her sorrow is deep—often sublimely deep; and a stranger intermeddles not with it. The hopes she formerly cherished are buried with the form that was once her joy and crown.

This wide world is hung with sackcloth;—and O! how empty show all its promises and joys! Often, too, pale Want is in attendance—and friends seem few—and health grows frail—and every pleasing prospect goes out in darkness. Now, then, is the hour, of all thy life, to reach out the trembling hand and touch the garment of thy God. Thy Maker is thy husband!

Ruth.

RUTH has been already introduced. She was a Moabitess, and became wife of Mahlon, one of the sons of Naomi, whose family, as we have seen, emigrated to Moab. After the death of the father and the two sons, and when the widowed mother had determined on returning to Judea, she earnestly entreated her daughters-in-law to return to their former homes, and permit her to return alone to her native country. Orpah sorrowfully acquiesced, and took her leave;—but no persuasions could induce Ruth to forsake her adopted mother. Her reply to the entreaties of that mother is stamped with perfect beauty, as well as propriety, and has been the admiration of all generations since. "Entreat me not to leave thee, or to return from following after thee; for whither thou goest I will go—and where thou lodgest I will lodge;—thy people shall be my people, and thy God, my God;—where thou diest will I die, and there will I be buried. The Lord do so to me, and more also, if aught but death part thee and me!"

What entire devotion is here exhibited! What daughter ever did more virtuously than this? How fully—how unreservedly, did she wed herself to all the fallen fortunes of the afflicted Naomi! And, what was better still, how cordially did she embrace the only true God! Whether, having been born and bred a heathen, she had become a proselyte in the house of her husband, does not appear. But in the decisive conversation with her mother-in-law, her adherence to the true religion is fully declared. Nor is there room for the slightest suspicion touching the simplicity and purity of motive by which this lovely daughter was actuated. She obviously loved, with a deep and quenchless love, her bereaved and sorrowful relative. Their sorrows, to some extent, had been one. The streams of their grief had met over the same graves—and over *one* especially. The soul of the child clave to the mother; and though every worldly prospect faded, yet refused to be separated. To the last day of time, will this devotion of Ruth the Moabitess be admired and praised. Millions of daughters will read and ponder the sweet accents whereby she vowed eternal adherence to her husband's mother; and as they weep with delight, will find their own filial affection and faithfulness confirmed and increased.

Ruth, with her mother, is at Bethlehem; and the second scene of her history is the scene of the harvest-field. Nor is it easy to conceive of a more enchanting picture of earthly beauty than what is here portrayed. There spreads out before the eye an extensive field of ripened grain, waving gracefully in the soft breezes of that lovely day. The reapers are abroad, and their track is marked by the shining rows of fallen grain stretching away in the distance. The maidens are also there—and they are wreathing the strong bands that are to inclose the swelling sheaves, while, at a little distance, is seen another, graceful, though poor—noble in bearing, though of pensive and modest aspect. Fairer days shone over her once. Though yet young and beautiful, she has drunk deep of the cup of bitterness. She has buried the one she loved—she is far away from her native fields and forests. She has come of late, a voluntary exile, to Judah's land, and has taken refuge beneath the wing of Judah's God. This morning, an unseen hand has led her to that harvest scene; and she has sought permission to glean behind the reapers, that she may gather the widow's scanty pittance.

Meanwhile, another one arrives; it is the wealthy and noble proprietor of the field. The joy of harvest is beaming from his countenance, as his eye rests upon the animated and brilliant scenery, and his mind is ascending to the God of providence, who has crowned the year with his goodness, and covered the valleys over with corn. "The Lord be with you!" is his salutation to the reapers. "The Lord bless thee!" is their joint and glad response. Well said, ye reapers! Your prayer is heard, and the blessing invoked for your master is already there, though he and you know not of it. "Whose damsel this?" he whispers, as he points to the beautiful gleaner. Was not that first glance the glance of love? That heart of goodness—is it not already trembling? Now the eye no longer follows the reapers, as with their shining sickles they gather the cumbrous grain. The maidens ply their lighter tasks unnoticed. That golden field is suddenly forgotten. An object more attractive than all harvest-scenes has riveted his eye, and his soul cleaves, though almost unconsciously, to this gentle, lovely stranger. Soft words succeed—the genuine accents of a heart whose great deep is stirred—which leaps forth to bless the charming object, but yet trembles at the first notes of its stifled voice. "Go not to glean in another field. No harm shall touch thee here. When thirsty, come and drink from the vessels. At meal-time, come and eat to the full. I have heard of thee, and of all thy sorrows and sacrifices. The Lord recompense thee abundantly! Ye reapers, deal kindly and generously with the gleaner!"

A high day was that to the gentle Ruth—and not for the much corn she gathered. At evening, bearing her treasure, she sought her beloved mother away in the city; and "the man's name" failed not to be spoken, that night, in their humble dwelling. More than once that name was blessed from the lips of Naomi; while, in her heart, deep thoughts were struggling, as, at the same moment, she spoke of Boaz, and glanced at her lovely daughter. Other days came on and passed, until the early and latter harvests were all gathered, nor, to the end, was Ruth seen to glean in "another field."

The scene of the threshing-floor next succeeds;—planned innocently, we must hope, by the provident Naomi,—executed innocently, we must hope, by the obedient daughter,—but to be imitated never! "My daughter, shall I not seek rest for thee, that it may be well with thee?" Amiable impulse! Nor need we doubt that in the soul of Ruth all was in readiness for such a "rest." Had she passed all those harvest-days in the fields of Boaz—and received so many kindnesses at his generous hands—and glanced so often upon that countenance that beamed naught upon her save love and goodness,—and was her heart untouched? Even in the earliest interview she said to him, "Thou hast comforted me." Might she not have added more, as time elapsed, and kind attentions multiplied? Tell me, ye who can guess, where, amid those days, were lingering the deep affections—the secret hopes of Ruth? If, on some day, the master of those harvest-fields tarried in Bethlehem, and came not to salute the reapers—was there not one spirit near by, to whom his absence was more painful than she wished to confess, even to herself? And when, at coming, he would bless the company, as usual, was not *one* response more deep and ardent than all the others, as it spoke tremblingly, "The Lord bless thee!"

Nor must we too hastily accuse her of advancing unbecomingly. There may have been—there doubtless were, circumstances associated with this strange interview, which we appreciate only with great difficulty. "Thou art my kinsman," steals on the ear of Boaz in the dark night. But it is a familiar voice—a voice of music to his soul—and the meaning was plain—and the hint was greatly welcome—and she knew it such—and the expected blessing was pronounced upon her.

Then follows the closing scene of this exquisite drama. "Sit still, my daughter;—the crisis comes," saith Naomi, as, laden with corn, the daughter returns from the mysterious colloquy. The prediction proves true. The man is "not in rest." All the necessary preliminaries are at once attended to, and, ere that day declines, Boaz and Ruth are one.

The record tells not to what needy ones those gleanings passed, now that the fair gleaner came to possess, so suddenly, the rich harvests themselves, and the owner thereof. Also, the brilliant happiness that awaited the daughter, and the consolation that fell to the mother, remain to be inferred. Ere yet another season of reaping had arrived, there nestled in the arms of Naomi an infant boy, born of the beautiful Ruth. That boy grew up to manhood, and his son's son was the great king and bard of Israel. And whoever shall trace the illustrious line running from Abraham to God's Messiah, will not fail to discern there the name of her who, though born an alien from the commonwealth of Israel, yet vowed to one of Israel's weeping daughters, "Thy God shall be my God!"

Hannah.

Few of the female characters of the Bible arise before us clothed with more interest and beauty than Hannah;—and there are few, from whose excellence so slight abatements are required to be made. Her position and history remind us of those of Rachel. Like her ancient sister, she was, unhappily, not *the wife*, but only *one* of the wives of her husband, Elkanah. Like Rachel, she was, however, the favorite wife; but also, like her, she was for some years childless, while her rival, Peninnah, was favored with sons and daughters. This advantage appears to have been ostentatiously and offensively abused by the unworthy Peninnah. Her proud and arrogant behavior, in her prosperity, toward the amiable

Hannah, in her humiliation, has stamped her name, so far as it is thought of at all, with undying infamy. She was as graceless as she was immodest—and as mean as she was ignorant and senseless—and as proud as she was hypocritical—and as wicked as she was audacious and disgusting. What seems more closely to ally a human being to a fiend, than to triumph over the unavoidable misfortunes of others? Nor can we wonder that, under such circumstances, the finely-wrought and sensitive spirit of Hannah was deeply troubled. It seemed sufficiently afflictive to endure the reproaches of her adversary when at home; and she had a right to expect, at least when abroad with strangers—and, most of all, when at the annual worship and sacrifice, and within sight of the ark of God—that she might be at peace. But when she perceived, from year to year, that these public and solemn occasions were specially selected as opportunities for pouring contempt upon her, she wept in the bitterness of her soul, and refused to be comforted by human sympathy.

"Whom the Lord loveth he correcteth;" and there are times when he deeply and painfully instructs such ones that all beneath is but shadow,—and whosoever leaneth there will but pierce himself through with many sorrows. Peter, as he sinks into the troubled and dark waters, can only lift his feeble hands aloft. There is no solid ground—every hope dies, save one; "Lord, save—I perish!" "Call upon me in the day of trouble, I will deliver thee!" is one of the dearest gems of the book of God. Here did the beloved Hannah feel herself at last to be shut up. In the anguish of her spirit, she "prayed unto the Lord." With many tears, and with holy vows, she begged of the Lord of hosts to look on her affliction, and to forget her not. As she prayed deeply and softly, the priest of God, while his eye fell upon her pale and sad countenance, her lips silent, yet speaking—mistook the agony of that prayer for the excitement of wine. "No, my lord! I am a woman of a sorrowful spirit. I have poured out my soul before the Lord, and out of the abundance of my complaint and grief have I spoken." The good priest pronounces his amen to her prayer, and then her tears are dried up, and her sadness passes away; and, having risen at early morning, and worshiped, and renewed her vows and thanksgivings, she returns, with her husband, to Ramah.

The next time Hannah went up to the house of the Lord in Shiloh, a lovely little child, her own son, accompanied her, to be lent, by his mother, to the Lord, according to the vows which she had made. She had called upon the great Helper, and her prayer was heard, and her reproach was taken away, and her heart exulted, and the pride and arrogance of her adversary were humbled to the dust. The song of Hannah, on this glad occasion, is full of exquisite beauty;

while, as a prophecy, it takes rank among the very first and loftiest of inspired compositions. Therein stands portrayed, in colors of surpassing sublimity, the glory of the Lord Jehovah. All other things are forgotten as He rises on the view. All other foundations disappear as he comes forth—the Everlasting Rock. All vanity and falsehood hide themselves before his dread omniscience. All destinies are in his hands, and at his bidding. The mighty and prosperous are brought down—and the desolate and fainting are revived and come forth, when he commands, to exceeding happiness and joy. The song swells and rises in its course—seizing upon still loftier strains, and, passing from the individual, it comprehends all nations, and sings of regal splendor yet to be;—while the glorious name—Messiah—swelling from the lips of Hannah, and spoken, by her, first on earth—strikes the ravished ear, and charms earth and heaven, as it forms the closing notes of one of the loveliest songs that was ever breathed in the hearing of mortals.

Hannah again returns to Ramah, having left at Shiloh—there to minister before the Lord—her consecrated boy. At every annual visit, as, in company with her husband, she went up to offer the yearly offering, she bears the "little coat," made by her hands, to adorn and comfort her beloved Samuel. There dwelt the lad—lent of his mother to Heaven—and grew, a fragrant plant, in the garden of the Lord. Doubtless his pleasant name was often heard in Ramah—while *one* was there, if no more, that daily spoke of him, as on the ear of the Eternal rose her songs of gratitude and rejoicing.

Meanwhile, new joys await the house of Hannah. She has lent to the Lord her child—her only one;—yet shall she not remain solitary. Other sons besides, and blooming daughters, rise up and call her blessed, who, in her affliction, sought after God, and trusted in him.

How full of instruction is the history of Hannah! Let the sorrowful remember where lives the great and inexhaustible Source of consolation. They may contemplate, in the mother of Samuel, a rich commentary upon the apostolic injunction, that if any is afflicted, he should pray. Let such forget not to carry *every* sorrow to the great Burden-bearer, and consider well that *he* is interested in whatever interests *them.* "Be careful for nothing: but in everything, by prayer and supplication, with thanksgiving, let your requests be made known unto God."

Study the history of Hannah, and then, ever afterwards, judge not according to the appearance, but judge righteous judgment. To the superficial eye, how disconsolate, in the midst of her sorrows, was Hannah;—how prosperous, in the midst of her boastings, was Peninnah! But count not that a curse which urges us to the Strong for help;—count not that, in effect, a blessing, wherein we forget our dependence, and

4*

dispense with goodness. True, Peninnah triumphed, for a day, amid her sons and daughters—and, in her prosperity, despised the solitary and weeping Hannah. But what of Peninnah? It is one of the mean and insignificant names written upon the Bible page, like as every true picture of earthly scenery must show some unsightly object. And what of her sons and daughters? No man knoweth their place or name. What now of Hannah? It is one of the names of beautiful and immortal fragrance; and often, to this day, it is heard amid the circles of Zion's lovely daughters,—allying to itself all pure and hallowed associations, and claiming to be grouped with such select names as that of Ruth, of Elizabeth, Anna, and Mary. And what of her son—her eldest born? It is a name great and most venerable;—renowned in the history of God's Providence — distinguished among the judges and prophets of Israel—and conspicuous among the priests of the Most High.

And speaks there no voice from Hannah to the mothers in Israel? As she lends that boy away to the Lord, is she in this to be counted, in no sense, as an example to her sisters of after generations? O! have Christian mothers no sons and daughters to lend to Christ? Have they, to this day, restrained their vows, or, having vowed, have they declined to fulfill, in good faith, the pledges they have made? Why should not every child of the Christian mother be counted, by her, as holy unto the Lord, and daily dedicated to him—and daily led where Jesus is—and feel, unceasingly, a holy atmosphere encompassing him—and be conducted by a soft, yet unyielding and constant influence, within the hallowed precincts of God's holy tabernacle? Mother! have you yet looked upon your son, and said, with Hannah, "As long as he liveth he shall be lent to the Lord?" And then, after that, did you always lend him accordingly—and, as often as you looked upon him, count him as lent—and always spake of him as such, when you talked with God—and always taught the child that he was lent to Christ—and always cherished him as a plant in God's sacred vineyard—and always imparted to him God's nurture—and trained him, every day, directly for immortality? Well, then, in after days, and "when he is old," he will be found walking there;—and, subsequently, in the heavenly circles, where will be seen Hannah and Samuel, there thou shalt greet thy own beloved offspring—once lent to Christ, and now restored to thee forever.

Abigail.

ABIGAIL rises before us as an example of a strong understanding, joined with great prudence. She was unequally yoked with a wealthy churl, Nabal by name, who resided in Maon, a few miles south of Hebron, and whose flocks were pastured in Carmel. At an annual sheep-shearing, David, then a fugitive from Saul, and sojourning in that vicinity, sent a deputation of ten young men to Nabal, to present, in their master's name, the salutations of peace, and to ask that, in the midst of his festivities and feasting, he would send, by the young men, a token of friendship, from whatever viands of the banquet might seem good to him. David, moreover, appears to have had some special claim upon Nabal, having essentially aided, during his stay in Carmel, in the protection of his flocks from depredation. Nabal, however, recognized no obligations to David, reciprocated not at all his courteous salutations, but sent back the deputation empty, and with highly contemptuous and insulting insinuations against him who had sent them. David immediately determined upon redress, and that, too, with summary and unjustifiable severity. Meanwhile, one of Nabal's men informed Abigail, his wife, touching the conduct of her husband to the messengers of David. Anticipating disastrous consequences, she, in great haste, proceeded to avert, if possible, the threatening ruin from the house of her husband; and taking a suitable offering, she, without his knowledge of her movements, hastens to David, and meets him at the foot of Carmel, as he was already on his way with four hundred men for the punishment of Nabal. Then follows the memorable address of Abigail to David, in which she confesses the great fault of her husband—asserts her own ignorance of the message that had been sent—beseeches him to accept the offering which she had brought—and, in the spirit of prophecy, announces her husband's fall, as well as the innocence, and certain victory and prosperity of David, and closes her speech with asking that she might not be forgotten when with him all should be well.

This strong and prophetic eloquence, coming, as it did, from a woman of uncommon beauty of countenance and behavior, accomplished the desired result, and was the means of averting a dreadful tragedy which, in the course of that night, would have sent to the shades many an innocent man, as well as the stupid Nabal.

Nor does this appear to have been the only effect of the timely interview between Abigail and David. His heart, as well as his mind and judgment, was deeply affected at the presence and bearing of this noble lady. His reply to her bespeaks strong emotion, as well as profound respect and consideration. He gives praise to God who had sent her to meet him. He pronounces his blessing upon the counsel which had been given him, and upon the fair prophetess who had uttered it, and who had thus preserved him from the intended slaughter;—and, after receiving her present, he dismissed her in peace—assuring her that he had complied with her wishes, and accepted her person.

Nabal, on being informed by his wife of the destruction that had been aimed at him, and from which, by her interference, he had barely escaped, seems to have been struck with consternation and amazement, from which he never recovered, and died, ten days afterward, by the judgment of God.

Thus a higher destiny opened before the intelligent and beautiful Abigail. However it may have been with her heart, there was no sorrow for David as he received intelligence of Nabal's demise. He remembered and loved the one whose eloquence and gracefulness had, a few days before, so won upon his heart, and from his hand a winged message of love speedily flies to the mansion of Abigail. Will the suspicion be pardoned, that such a message was expected? As, a few days since, she stood before that mighty man, did her purified vision behold for him "a sure house"—enemies vanquished—himself the approved ruler over Israel—the forthcoming decease of Nabal? With these visions before her, and as she closed her speech, asking for herself a kind remembrance, was there no impression, meanwhile, of any connection of these great matters with her own future position?

Her modest and becoming response to the important message is not forgotten; nor that she hasted, and, with her damsels, came, like Rebecca, and greeted and wedded the royal bridegroom.

After this but little is written. One son was born to her after her marriage with David. She shared the affections of her husband, at first, with Abinoam, a previous wife; while, not long afterward, we hear of other wives still in the king's residence. Hence, how much the happiness of her life was advanced by her new position, may be a matter of uncertainty and doubt. Yet it is refreshing, that while, in her, we are permitted to discern uncommon prudence and strength of understanding, combined, also, with piety of heart, and much personal grace and beauty, no reproach attaches itself to the name of Abigail.

Bathsheba.

"No reproach attaches itself to the name of Abigail." Not so, alas! with her whose name introduces the present chapter. The only pleasant thing that is written of her is, that "the woman was very beautiful to look upon." But how little is this, if it be all! Even this is only melancholy, if, as in the case before us, it prove but the occasion of temptation, diaster, and ruin. No student of the Holy Scriptures ever feels any special love for Bathsheba. In the absence of all allusion to any intellectual or moral excellence, her exterior charms are well-nigh unthought of. Her name is never recalled without dragging along with it associations such as we would fain shut away forever. Apostasy—impurity—conjugal infidelity—deceit—meanness—murder—the curse—such is the frightful category that groups itself inseparably with the name of Bathsheba—spoiling it as with the serpent's slime, and setting it aside, like the leprous garment, from whatever is healthy, innocent, and pure. True, there is pity mingled with our profound disapprobation. In excluding her from the circles of goodness, we are not conscious of those feelings of detestation which arise with all our recollections of Delilah. We fail to discern that settled and deep depravity—that determined and heartless iniquity, so characteristic of the woman of Sorek. We think of Bathsheba as slender in virtue, rather than as strong in vice. We contemplate her as a negative in respect to true goodness, instead of as a positive in respect to moral deformity. Previous to the fatal evening, we hardly suspect any misconduct in the wife of Uriah. In those days her husband was away in the wars, valiant among the hosts of Israel, and his wife, meanwhile, at her pleasant home on Mount Zion, was innocent; and, in the day of her fall, it may be, she thought of nothing so improbable as her infidelity to the brave man to whom she was lawfully and virtuously joined. This, to be sure, is conjecture; but it is an irresistible impression left upon the writer's mind, from careful meditation of all that is recorded. We are ashamed of her where the royal glance first meets her. In our indignation, we exclaim, with withering emphasis, that that ceremony should have been elsewhere;—that if, in selecting that situation, she was careless, it was a criminal carelessness—if she was wicked, it was hateful wickedness. Yet, if we assume the milder hypothesis, and charge her that on that evening she cherished no fell intent, but was only guilty of cruel and disgraceful negligence, then the greater sin involved in the catastrophe will be charged to another than to Bathsheba. That was the greater sinner who, after all God's wondrous dealings in his behalf, and being gifted with extraordinary powers of mind and body, and standing, by Divine appointment, at the head of a great and mighty people, and attracting to himself the eyes of all his subjects, as well as of many nations around, and of the angels above him, and seeing fairer prospects rising before him than what had ever glowed before fallen beings—he was the greater sinner who, embraced by circumstances so sublime, so restraining, should, with one fell swoop, cut so deliberately the golden cords that bound him to the great universe of purity and goodness, and go down to take his place with the filth and offscouring of the race, and join cordial hands with the foul debauchee, the deceiver, the robber, the murderer! I confess that I recollect but few crimes in the bloody history of our race, which, under all the circumstances, were so profoundly black, and disgusting, and frightful, as the great crime of David. It is worse than idle to disguise or palliate it. Let it appear in its whole deformity before an astonished world; and let that world stand more astonished still, as it hears the voice of boundless grace exclaiming to this strange sinner, "I have put away thy sin!"

We trust the preceding suggestions may hint that we feel no disposition to deal unkindly with Bathsheba. When, on the evening of the fatal eclipse, the message reached her that her presence was desired within the royal residence, it is difficult for us to appreciate all the circumstances that weighed upon her too fragile mind. There meets her that night, and in that apartment, a great and mighty king. He is, withal, noble and beautiful in person; and his fame is great for goodness, as well as for wealth, dignity, bravery, and power. None of all the earth is equal to him. *Can such a one do wrong?* But enough! Bathsheba falls;—but there are some palliations. Righteousness utters decisive condemnation,—while Pity sits by, and weeps for the desolate.

How sudden, and how great the change! When did ever misery fail to follow close upon the heels of crime? Sin, when it is finished, bringeth forth death. Yesterday, all was innocence and sunny peace. To-day the sky is overcast, and distant and awful thunders portend fearful tempests and ruin. Either the brave Uriah; or else his guilty wife, with, perhaps, the partner of her sin, must perish. The noble soldier, of course, dies—and Bathsheba passes speedily up to the arms of royalty. She rises thither, but not to be happy. No smiling Providence had invited her coming. It was a frightful passage as she hastened. The shrieks of the murdered were in her ear—and pools of blood were beneath her feet—and ghastly spectres were hovering near,—and pure angel beings had retired hence—and the demon Shame hissed as she entered the royal gates. And treading those splendid apartments, Peace never met her there. The Sword dwelt there—and Death came often—and, now and then, cries of deepest agony echoed through those halls; and the night when Bathsheba fell was with her the beginning of sorrows.

She survived her husband, the king of Israel, and saw her son established upon the throne of his father. He was a son of promise—virtuous and lovely in his youth, as we may hope his mother was, before yet he had begun to be. Yet he, too, resigned his integrity, and never did so bright a morning go out in so mournful a darkness. The fall of Solomon seemed the sad echo of the disaster of Bathsheba—was permitted, perchance, as one of the judicial visitations of Heaven—and grew, for aught we know, by natural process, from seeds whose springing and whose fruit are far too sure and certain.

The moral of Bathsheba's history urges the young of her sex to cultivate the sternest integrity of moral principle—and the utmost beauty of character—and perfect modesty of movements and manners. It reminds them to beware of doubtful influences breathing upon them from high places—to settle it well that nothing—nothing can supply the loss of goodness—that while the lonely cottage where Christ and innocence abide, is next to heaven—the palace, with all its luxury and gold, if guilt be there, is but the brilliant haunting-place of woe.

Queen of Sheba.

It falls not within the purpose of these brief sketches to concern with uninspired and varying speculations touching the characters coming under notice;—but to confine ourselves, rather, to the simple presentation of Scripture, and avail ourselves mainly of the hints afforded there from which to derive any observations of instruction or interest.

Solomon, among other enterprises of importance, appears to have carried on an extensive commerce with Ophir, a tropical country, situated, as is probable, on the eastern coast of Africa, and judged, by Mr. Bruce, to have been the same with Arabia or Sheba, of which the subject of this sketch was the sovereign in the time of Solomon. The vast quantities of gold, precious stones, and trees imported by the king of Israel from that country, and his great fame, which had, of course, amid so much commercial intercourse, reached the ears of the queen, very naturally excited a strong curiosity to see and hear him. So deeply interested was she in this matter, that notwithstanding the great distance, and other difficulties which, in her case, must have had existence, she undertook the journey to Jerusalem. Her equipage was princely, and suitable to a person of her distinction, while her presents which she had prepared for king Solomon were, in the highest degree, magnificent and valuable. Her visit appears to have proved entirely satisfactory to herself. The great wisdom of Solomon, and the boundless wealth and splendor of the temple and court, filled her with amazement;—so that ample as her expectations were, from the reports she had received at home, they were all more than realized by a personal visit and examination.

Several things have been conjectured of this illustrious queen, and her renowned visit to the Jewish court, some of which appear to be not specially eulogistic of her character. All these we may easily afford to forget, while we hasten to view her through that medium which, so far as it may be used, is unerring.

It is thus that we are inclined to infer for the queen of Sheba a pure and exalted motive and conduct in her visit to the king of Israel. Was it a mere idle curiosity by which she was actuated? Or was it some lower motive still? Permit the inspired hand to write the true answer to all such inquiries. "When the queen of Sheba heard of the fame of Solomon concerning the name of the Lord, she came to prove him with hard questions." It was not, then, merely that he was *famous*, that she desired to see him and commune with him, but the great consideration that he was *famous concerning the name of the Lord.* Here is the key by which we are to open to view the character of this illustrious woman;—

and the truth it reveals is a thousand-fold more—and a thousand-fold more precious, than of all unwarrantable speculations. The queen of Sheba was either already a person of true piety, or desirous of becoming so. She came from far to hear concerning the Lord. She came, for the fame of Solomon's wisdom had excited within her heart unusual hopes. She came with large expense, and, probably, at great sacrifices. She came with a mind adorned not only with great intelligence and acuteness, but intent upon the lofty purpose of her visit. She may have been a Jewess; or, having been a Pagan, she may have learned, by her intercourse with the traders from Judea, concerning the true God, and of the mode of seeking and worshiping him. Be all this as it may, she desired, with a great desire, to know the Lord more fully, while here centered all her inquiries which she presented to Solomon. There were questions with which her active and intelligent mind found difficulty; and yet were they questions of great importance, and for the solution of which she would not, and did not, hesitate to go a great distance. Had this woman, with the same mind and spirit, lived in the time of Christ, and had heard by report, as the Jews heard directly, of his wisdom, she would have taken equal and greater pains to learn "concerning the name of the Lord," from the lips of Him who was so much greater than Solomon.

And the importance, as well as the propriety of

her inquiries may be rationally inferred from the result. "Not anything was hid from the king which he told her not." The Lord gave him the requisite wisdom;—nothing "was hid" from him, that he might communicate to her all the instruction that was necessary or desirable. So also may the drift of her intentions, and the character of her heart, be very clearly and satisfactorily discerned in the effect produced upon her mind by her intercourse with Solomon, and in her pious as well as dignified address to him. Not content with congratulating those whose privilege it was to be constantly near him, and listen to his wisdom, she adds most elegantly, "Blessed be the Lord thy God which delighted in thee, to set thee on the throne of Israel, because the Lord loved Israel forever; therefore made he thee king to do judgment and justice." Three things must not fail to be detected here. The queen of Sheba is assured that the Lord loved Israel forever. What is this but faith? Secondly, she praises the God who loved Israel. What is this but love? Lastly, she recognizes judgment and justice, while, with consummate skill, she reminds and persuades Solomon to exercise them in his kingdom. What is this but righteousness? Faith—love—righteousness—"these three" were all thine, noble and most excellent queen of the South! Such wast thou as thy farewell was given to Israel, and thou returnedst to "the uttermost parts of the earth!"

A Divine voice, that spake as never man spake,

deduced for us the moral—a momentous lesson—of the history of the queen of Sheba. She "shall rise in the judgment to condemn this generation; for she came from the uttermost parts of the earth to hear the wisdom of Solomon; and behold, a greater than Solomon is here." Thus said Christ to the hardened Jews. Gentle reader! Has this no application to thee? She traversed a long and weary distance—she devoted much time and abundant treasure—to hear the wisdom of Solomon. Do you learn of Christ? And his wisdom is far greater;—and he is near you;—and to know him is eternal life!

Widow of Sarepta.

THERE was hanging over the land of Israel one of those awful judgments which the God of providence saw to be often necessary, in order to remind that stiffnecked people of their duty, and lead them back from that idolatry to which, previous to the captivity, they were so strangely liable. The prayer of Elijah had shut up the heavens, and the frightful famine was abroad. The Sidonian widow was gathering a few sticks with which to bake her last loaf for herself and little son, that they might eat it and die. "Bring me, I pray thee, a morsel of bread," utters a stranger's voice. Her heart sunk within her, for that voice fell on her ear with an unwonted authority, as it seemed to demand her last morsel. "Fear not," adds the mysterious stranger; "provide for me, and afterwards for thyself and son; for thy jar and cruise shall not fail, till the famine be ended." The widow believed, and, in her extremity, she divided her bread with the weary and famishing prophet. The word of the Lord failed her not; her giving was her receiving—and it was good measure, pressed down, and running over. There is a beautiful Providence that can extract life from death itself, and reveal the honeycomb, even amid the decaying carcass. Abundance was the widow's allotment henceforth, for "many days;"—yet shadows will pass over the most favored, and gloom again settles upon the humble mansion of the widow of Sarepta. That little son falls sick;—and his sickness is dreadful, and his breath departs. In this world great griefs will come, and there are times when they will come suddenly. Blessed are they who then possess their souls in patience, and remove not their hand from the great Father's. In the wildness of the widow's sorrow, she glances upon the good prophet, as though he had come to bring judgment to her house, rather than mercy, and as if his hand were concerned in the death of her boy. "Art thou come to call my sin to remembrance, and to slay my son?" Be not in haste to speak, especially when deep distress overshadows thee, and when the agony of disappointment and grief presses thee deeply to the dust. Weep softly, and let thy heart bleed in silence. Or if thy lips be opened—if thy cries must be uttered, let it be rather in the ear of God, that is open to prayer. There is hazard when, in such awful times, we glance elsewhere than upon heaven. The aching eye is often dim and confused. It may seem to discern enemies when only friends are near. It may think to detect secondary agencies, and be blind to the great hand that holds and directs all destinies. "It is the Lord," is Faith's solemn voice;—and then the spirit, in its bitterness, is hushed and still,—and cold suspicion dies—and the heart is at peace with all men, and with itself—and "Blessed be the name of the Lord!" is the song of the weeping.

And often, too, there is provided a way of escape. The walls of darkness may seem impenetrable, and the last hope may seem to give way—when, all suddenly, the cloud heaves up, and we look for it, and lo! it is gone;—and skies spread themselves over us, such as are more beautiful and brilliant than we had gazed upon before—and the night is spent, and the day is come. Great is God; and as good and merciful as he is great. He pities the widow, and often remembers her tears, when human sympathies are feeble and few. "O Lord my God!" cries the prophet, "I pray thee let this child's soul come into him again!" It is a sublime prayer. A man on earth goes feeling after a soul resident in eternity; and the God of infinite sympathy helps, and the departed spirit is permitted to return. "See, thy son liveth!" saith the prophet, as he restores the lad to his astonished and rejoicing mother. Those eyes are animated and brilliant once more. The paleness of death has left those features, and the lips that just now appeared sealed forever, open and speak again.

From that day, the widow of Sarepta trusted in the God of Elijah. "The word of the Lord is truth!" she exclaimed, and as she believed, it was counted to her for righteousness. "Blessed are all they that put their trust in Him!"

"Be not forgetful to entertain strangers, for thereby some have entertained angels unawares."

Such appears to be the moral of what is written of the Sidonian widow. Too often is the stranger, as he enters our doors, counted as unwelcome. The world is shut out—and the little circle is quiet now. A chosen company are there; and smiles, and joyous converse, and pleasant fruits, and delicious music, gladden the scenery. "Far off be the stranger;—nor may he intermeddle with those hours of brilliancy!" Or, there may be a different aspect. The dwelling may be cold and cheerless—and the widow and the orphan may be lingering there—and want and sorrow dwell there—and cries for bread from helpless ones pierce often that poor mother's heart,—and Hope has fled away, for the last loaf is prepared, and the last scanty meal is made ready, that they may eat and die. "Far off be the stranger!" Yet pray not thus too ardently, daughter of sadness! And if he come—come to share thy last pittance—grieve not too sorely. He may be God's messenger; he may be to thee some angel of mercy, commissioned to bear to thy cheerless mansion abundance instead of famine, and life rather than death.

"Although the vine its fruit deny,
Although the olive yield no oil,
The withering fig-trees droop and die,
The fields elude the tiller's toil,
The empty stall no herd afford,
And perish all the bleating race,—
Yet will I triumph in the Lord,
The God of my salvation praise!"

Jezebel.

This is, perhaps, the most hateful of the female characters exhibited in the sacred Scriptures. She was of royal descent, being daughter of the king of Tyre; and having been bred a Pagan, she remained a confirmed idolatress to the day of her death. Ahab, one of the most wicked of Israel's kings, sought and obtained her hand, and introducing his heathen wife to his court and people, he also led in her idolatry, became himself a worshiper of Baal, and established the heathen altars and priesthood in all his kingdom. Four hundred and fifty prophets of Baal were scattered through his dominions, and four hundred, besides, priests of the impure rites of the Sidonian Astarte, were supported constantly at the table of the infamous Jezebel. Meanwhile, the prophets of the Lord were everywhere persecuted and slain at her command, and the true worship was interdicted, and substituted by the abominations of heathenism.

The great Elijah, amid these troublous times, was, of course, a doomed man, and his life was especially sought by the wicked Ahab and Jezebel. He saw the frightful apostasies of the kingdom of Israel, and his prayer had gone up to God for the withholding of the rains of heaven, in order that, by the judgments of the Almighty upon the land, the inhabitants thereof might learn righteousness. Dreadful famine, as a consequence, was prevailing; but the king and queen, like Pharaoh of Egypt, were only hardened, rather than subdued, by the judicial visitation; while their vengeance waxed hotter and hotter against God and his people.

Elijah at length comes forth from his hiding-places, and shows himself to Ahab, who hails him as the troubler of Israel. With tremendous emphasis the prophet retorts the charge upon the king, and, with his characteristic fearlessness, proclaims to him the sad cause of all the wide-spread calamity. "Thou, and thy father's house, have forsaken the commandment of the Lord, and have followed Balaam." The great demonstration at Mount Carmel succeeds, and the true God is again acknowledged by the assembled multitude, and the prophets of Baal die by Elijah's hand, and again his prayer ascends, and the "heavens gave rain." It would seem that the whole nation, together with their idolatrous rulers, must now be certainly convinced, and that the true and righteous Jehovah would be recognized and honored. So, probably, thought Elijah. But if so, he was speedily undeceived. That mighty rain had yet scarcely ceased to fall—the first for three years and six months—ere the prophet receives a message from the hand of Jezebel, threatening his immediate death. The voice of God was as if sounding in her ears, as her malignant notes were thundering in the ears of his faithful prophet. Was there ever such a lesson touching the depth of human wickedness when the heart is fully set to do evil!

Elijah retires hastily from the reach of the hateful queen, and she sees him no more. Her course is still downward and bloody. The unfortunate Naboth perishes by her instigation, and Ahab, "whom Jezebel, his wife, stirred up," sold himself to work wickedness beyond all men. He died, at last, as all bad men must die. Jezebel survived her husband about thirteen years, and died by violence at the command of Jehu, and her body was eaten of dogs.

The history of this heathen queen is only melancholy. It is darkness without light. As we contemplate it, we seem in a world of demons rather than of beings that are human. The soul grows sick, and shudders at what one of our fallen race may become. What! can man—especially can woman, sink, in this world, to degradation so extreme and awful? Well may we weep over sin, and flee from it as from the fell serpent's fangs. Well may we tremble at the dire ravages of heathenism—effacing, as it does, the image of God from the soul, scathing whatever is beautiful to behold, and transforming man or woman into a fiend of darkness. Well may Christian mothers and daughters lay themselves out for the redemption of their Pagan sisters, and aid, to the utmost, in bearing to them that only remedy for the moral desolations of the race. Jezebel was a heathen, and a representative of heathenism—a monument of what a thousand Christian women, without redemption, would be, who are now the loveliest ornaments of this world, and almost "as the angels of God in heaven."

"Shall we, whose souls are lighted
With wisdom from on high,
Shall we, to souls benighted,
The lamp of life deny?
Salvation! O salvation!
The joyful sound proclaim,
Till earth's remotest nation
Has learn'd Messiah's name!"

The Shunammite.

"ELISHA passed to Shunem where was a great woman;"—distinguished for excellence of character and conduct; for such are they who are great in the sight of the Lord. She appears to have possessed an ardent temperament, which imparted to her beneficence an earnestness of cordiality beyond what is ordinary. Elisha would seem to have been residing, for a time, in the vicinity, while his calls of duty often led him to pass her dwelling. It would not be strange if, as she now and then glanced at the man of God passing her residence, she observed him to be weary and faint with his journeyings; and hence her goodness of heart prompted her earnest invitation that he would accept and enjoy her hospitalities. Having made her acquaintance, and realized her kindness, her residence became a favored and favorite resting-place of the prophet. And more prophets than one have found occasion for lofty gratitude, as they have been refreshed by the cheering smiles, and generous sympathies, of some intelligent and excellent daughter of Zion. Long after Elisha and his noble hostess of Shunem had passed away, the great apostle of the Gentiles often rejoiced in the house of Lydia, and was succored by the kind attentions of Phebe. In the house of Priscilla,

Apollos the eloquent not only found refreshment and repose, but also learned, at her lips, "the way of God more perfectly." The "elect lady" was greatly beloved by John, who was often welcomed to her house, and with her had conversed with fullness of joy. One of the mansions of Bethany was a favored resting-place of the Man of sorrows, who loved Martha, and her sister, and Lazarus. This thorny world shall not be utterly a desert while such are scattered here and there to bloom upon its surface, and cheer, with their fragrance, the weary traveler.

There seems an elegant exuberance in the sympathy of the Shunammite, as well as admirable prudence and discernment. Her generous hospitality is not satisfied with contemplating merely ordinary arrangements. She would have a room constructed and fitted up specially for the man of God, whither, at his pleasure, he might retire to meditate, and pray, and repose. Nor did she proceed with arrangements so important without the co-operation of her husband. "Behold now," she said to him, "I perceive that this is a holy man of God which passeth by us continually." And such discernment of hers, reveals to us, in part, her own fair and excellent character. She was not as the heath, knowing not when good cometh, but her senses were exercised to know good and evil. She could discern the character of the prophet; and, discerning it, could sympathize with its sublimity and beauty. Piety and goodness had no repulsiveness in her eye, but irresistible attraction rather. She was not content that they should "pass continually" by her —she invited their presence, and wished them to linger with her, and welcomed them with the warmest cordiality. It is refreshing to observe, also, her interest to inspire the same sentiments in her husband. She would have been greatly distressed to be doomed, without his acquiescence and pleasure to carry out her plans for the prophet's entertainment and comfort. She seeks that there be but one mind—one thought, in those whom God had joined together. Nor is she obtrusive, while she is forward in her plans of goodness. There is no stepping aside from the sweet proprieties of woman. She was "great," yet not imperious and haughty—not selfish and secluded. "Let us make a little chamber, I pray thee, on the wall." On the one hand, she would do all possible for the comfort of the prophet; on the other, she is equally solicitous for her husband's sympathy in her benevolent projects. Those projects are successfully fulfilled, and the messenger of Heaven failed not to honor the prophet's chamber with his presence.

"The Lord give mercy to the house of Onesiphorus; for he often refreshed me." Thus prayed an apostle for one of the circles that were privileged to minister to his necessities. In like manner prayed Elisha as he was once reposing in that little chamber made upon the wall. And who may compute the results of such a petition? The effectual fervent prayer of a righteous man availeth much. "Call this Shunammite!" The prophet has prayed, and the response would seem to have been, that he select his blessing for the favored woman. She has come, at his command, and is standing before him. "Behold," he saith, "thou hast been careful—very careful for me;—what is to be done for thee?" It was no earthly recompense that, in her kindness and beneficence, had been sought for by this elegant lady; yet such a recompense is suddenly proffered. "Wilt thou be named to the king?" Shall great favor come to her from the throne, or the camp? Would she wish to pass up and tread in high places, and mingle in the brilliant circles of the court? "I dwell among mine own people," is the reply of her to whose greatness inspiration itself hath borne testimony. What was the pomp and glory of the world to her, whose eye was reposing upon a far more glorious destiny, and who was laboring not for the meat that perisheth? Nor does she give further answer to the prophet's inquiry. She was looking for no special reward of her goodness to an eminent servant of the Most High. Her privilege was her reward—and she deemed it a high honor to lie at his feet, and be permitted to provide for his necessities; while, with her brief and characteristic response to the prophet, she again disappears. But the man of

God is not at rest. "A blessing must come to this house. What, then, is to be done for her?" Such is the burden of a heart oppressed with holy gratitude and affection. It must bless that it may itself be refreshed.

The woman of Shunem becomes a mother. When five or six summers pass away, her little son, like that of the Sidonian widow, droops and perishes. Elijah, who had comforted the widow in her bereavement, had, long since, passed away to heaven in a chariot of fire, yet his mantle, as he rose, fell upon Elisha, to whom was now hastening, in her affliction, his distinguished hostess. She had laid away the little corpse upon the prophet's bed, and, turning her face toward Carmel, she drove swiftly. Afar off, the man of God, as he stood aloft, marked her rapid approach. "Is it well with thee—thy husband—thy child?" "It is well!" and her trembling hands are seizing the prophet's feet, and the tears of her sorrow are gushing swiftly and bitterly.

Yet, ere nightfall, this storm passes over, and there is brightness and brilliancy again, like the clear shining after rain. Another spirit comes back from eternity at the call of a man, and the little corpse is reanimated, and rises up from the prophet's bed; and she who, in the morning, sought that room with mourning, came thither again, at evening, to embrace joy and rejoicing.

"She rear'd a simple cloister there,
And placed its artless furniture;
And welcomed oft the man of prayer
Within the house she made so sure.

"And oft the weary prophet sought
Repose within those peaceful walls—
The quietness that lingers not
In folly's gay and noisy halls.

"That room was blesséd!—it was there
He ask'd, 'What shall be done for thee?'
And beauteous visions open'd where
She deck'd that bower thus gracefully.

"There once she wept, indeed; 'twas when,
Softly upon the prophet's bed,
She laid her boy; then sobb'd again,
And left him there all pale and dead.

"Yet joy illumed again, at even,
The 'little chamber on the wall,'
Where to her arms that boy was given,
Waked by the great Elisha's call.

"I'll write it, then, with scenes of bliss,
Such as the soul shall long remember;
And, in my heart, will often kiss
The hand that rear'd that prophet's chamber."

The "Little Maid."

MAY we not consent to notice what the Divine pen has condescended to distinguish by an eternal memorial?

And why, then, should we forget the little captive maid in the house of Naaman? It is true, we hear little of her. She was one of the victims of cruel and relentless war; and, by one of those sudden invasions by which the Syrians were accustomed to vex the neighboring kingdom of Israel, this little daughter of misfortune was taken captive, conveyed to Damascus, and became waiting-maid to the wife of Naaman.

She was, probably, a native of Samaria, inasmuch as she was so familiar with the fact of Elisha's residence there. How long she had been a captive we are not informed; nor whether her family and kindred were still living; or whether her parents, and others of her relatives, perished when she was torn away from her childhood's home; or whether they were also captives in some other region of Syria. We find her alone in the house of the Syrian captain. Yet she had not been long there; for she, though young, yet remembers her native country and city, and distinguished characters which she has seen or heard of there. Of course, she was capable of deep sorrow on account of her enslaved condition, and, doubtless, often wept as she remembered her distant and beloved home, and the mother whom she would see no more, and all the beloved companions of her happy childhood.

Yet she is not overcome by her sorrows. We regard her as possessing a fortitude and composure highly becoming for one so young and frail. There are obvious, also, a decided affection for her master and mistress, and interest for their welfare. "Would God my lord were with the prophet that is in Samaria! for he would recover him of his leprosy." These beautiful words are all we are permitted to hear from this dear captive child. Yet these speak much; for they tell of strong and earnest solicitude for the health and comfort of her master. She does not merely communicate the fact of a mighty prophet in Samaria. Such communication would be characteristic of a mind rising but a slight degree above indifference. Thus was not the "little maid." The intelligence she imparts takes the form of an earnest wish or prayer. It is the outbreaking of an affectionate and devoted heart —a heart overlooking all injuries of which she may have been the subject in the matter of her enslavement, and forcible detention from the scenes of her nativity.

Her language bespeaks her intelligence, as well as her sympathy and goodness. She was a little maid, slight in stature, and of tender years; yet her speech is mature. She knew the great prophet, and speaks of him with all the assurance of full intelligence and unwavering confidence. "He would recover him of his leprosy." That was much to know, and much to say. Yet was it so known, and so said, as to claim authority, and produce conviction,—and that, too, upon superior minds. "Thus and thus said the maid," the Syrian king was told. And the king was moved, and the letter of introduction is prepared, directed to the monarch of Israel; and the "great and honorable captain"—the "mighty man of valor," is presently on his way to Samaria, with splendid equipage and magnificent presents. That little voice, and those few words—few, yet effective—produce great movements.

And there is no ultimate disappointment. The great captain returns to his wife, and to the little maid, a renewed being—renewed first, in body, his flesh as that of a little child,—and renewed in mind and spirit, offering thereafter, no sacrifice, save to the true God, and bearing as he comes the great prophet's blessing.

It seems safe, then, to infer a better destiny for the captive child. Health, piety, happiness, and life, had all come, through her agency, to the great man her master. Did he not bless her, then, as he returned with joy from the prophet's presence? Found she not again her native home? And were riches and honor withheld from her whose fair wishes for her master's welfare were but the prelude of their full accomplishment?

Be her memory then forever lovely! Her voice was delicious music, and the outbreathing of her lips was health and fragrance. Her words were full of modesty and discretion—and they were "winged words"—and their echo was as protracted as it was beautiful. "Would my lord were with the prophet!" He was promptly with the prophet. "He would heal him!" He did heal him.

The moral of the story touching the "little maid" is this:—That a child—a little captive one—may, by a "fitly spoken" word, perform a good whose influence shall be incalculable and everlasting.

Vashti.

VASHTI was wife of Ahasuerus, king of Persia—who was the same as Artaxerxes, son of the famous Xerxes. That period of her history of which we have an account in the Scriptures, was four hundred and sixty years before the birth of Christ. Sacred and profane history both assign to her husband an extensive and mighty empire, reaching from India on the east to Ethiopia west, and embracing one hundred and twenty-seven provinces. Such was the great dignity of Vashti, whose beauty and accomplishments appear to have been correspondent with her lofty position. In the third year of her husband's reign, extraordinary festivities were ordered by him, in his palace at Shushan, where, during one hundred and eighty days, he entertained all the princes and nobility of his numerous provinces, and displayed before them the exuberant riches and splendor of his kingdom. At the end of the hundred and fourscore days, he ordered another feast for the people of the city, which continued seven days; and during the same time Queen Vashti made a feast for the women, in accordance with the oriental custom of the separation of the sexes on such occasions.

On the closing day of this latter feast, and when the king was "merry with wine," he sends his seven chamberlains to conduct the queen, in full array of royalty, to the presence of the king, in order that he might exhibit to the assembled nobility and people her extraordinary beauty. The queen refused compliance with the king's requisition, and, as a consequence, with the advice and counsel of his wise men, she was divorced from her husband—was deprived of the royal dignity, and another ascended to occupy the position which she had forfeited.

After this there is no more related of Vashti; nor is there necessity for anything further. Enough is written to illustrate the perfect propriety of her conduct, as well as the consummate injustice she was compelled to receive at the hands of her graceless husband. All those aspects of Vashti's character which we are permitted to discern, are becoming and beautiful. We observe a decorous cordiality and sympathy in the festivities which, on this great occasion, were ordered by the king. We perceive her readiness to associate with him in the feast of seven days to the people of Shushan, and, in accordance with the Persian customs, to entertain the mothers and daughters, while the king should provide the banquetings for the fathers and sons. She exhibits herself as prompt to every act of propriety and courtesy. She was one with her royal consort, so long as he was self-possessed and rational. She was obedient, as was meet, while the king was worthy of her obedience. But when, after long wine-drinking, he became intoxicated, and was no longer a man, and reason was dethroned, and virtue was prostrate, and the commands of his lips became but as the babblings of insanity,—then, most appropriately and righteously, she declined his requirements. What virtuous princess of modern kingdoms would not, in similar circumstances, imitate her noble example?

There are several considerations that challenge our respect and love for this beautiful queen of Persia.

We respect and love her for her dignity. She was a distinguished personage, and stood in a distinguished position. Few women were ever more elevated in rank or station. With a proper appreciation of her position and duty, she justly scorned to be placed on exhibition, and exposed to the rude gaze of a bacchanalian host, with the prince of bacchanals at their head, and acting as master of ceremonies. What respect, after such a degrading ceremony, could she have ever retained for herself—her husband—or her station?

We respect and love her for her modesty and humility. A vain and ostentatious lady might, with little hesitation, have complied with the royal command. She might have been prompt, despite of all impropriety or disgrace, to seize such an opportunity for the proclamation and display of her charms. But nothing like this was the character of this noble woman. She possessed beauty—peerless beauty of person; for she stood at the head of her sex throughout that vast kingdom—a position for which personal elegance appears to have been a capital test of qualification. Had she been vain, rather than virtuous—and ostentatious, rather than modest, what a rare opportunity was now presented for the gratification of her ambition! But such a ceremony was utterly distasteful. She chose to bloom in retirement, and counted the cruel exposure to which she was cited, to be but the sad blighting of her charms, and the eclipsing of all her brilliancy.

We respect and love her for her disinterestedness. The sacred narrative, with its characteristic brevity, forbears to admit us into the more private halls of that splendid palace. We are not permitted to look upon Vashti, as she receives the shameful message to prepare herself to stand as a public spectacle. The struggle which for a moment agitated that delicate and accomplished mind, is not revealed. Yet it is quite easy to guess what she must have clearly foreseen. When she consented to disobey the great monarch of Persia, she knew full well that the consequences would be momentous; and together with her decision to decline, she decided also to relinquish her fair station, and even to submit to death itself. To one, if not both of these melancholy results, she saw she would be doomed, and still "she refused to come at the king's commandment." Honor to her! She therein demonstrated before the eyes of that vast nation, as well as to all after generations, that she was as noble as she was beautiful; and that the greatness of her mind, and the refinement of her heart, were entirely commensurate with the enchanting gracefulness of her person.

Thus do we presume to estimate this proscribed and unfortunate lady,—if, indeed, it should be reckoned a misfortune that so much loftiness and excellence should become emancipated from so much meanness and mire. Immeasurably too lovely and good was such a queen to be linked, in her destinies, with a purling drunkard—king though he might be. The heart of sympathy could wish that she might never have entered that palace, to be insulted by the presence of besotted royalty, and sickened by the breath of magnificent beastliness. Would she might have bloomed still in the vales of peacefulness, and wedded there the brilliant counterpart of her own inestimable beauty, dignity, and worth! Too good was she for a king—too noble for a palace—too virtuous for a court—too beautiful for a crown.

Whither Vashti retired, when she "came no more before king Ahasaerus," there is no record. She saw another rise up to take her place and wear the crown which had been unrighteously torn from her own head. It is pleasant that no other harm is discovered ; and pleasant to believe that self-respect, a good conscience, peace and quietness, attended her who, by her virtue, and not by her fault and vice, was compelled to lay off the comfortless vestments of royalty.

Christianity enjoins upon the wife obedience to her husband ; yet guards her, in this matter, with strong limitations. That husband is to love his wife—love her as his own flesh. In other words, he is never to tyrannize over her,—never to be unkind,—never unreasonable,—never require what is wrong, indecorous, or improper ; while his very commands—if, indeed, he ever utters any to his wife—are to be but the outbreathings of kindness and love. If, then, with a spirit the reverse of all this, he demands of his wife, as of a servant, to do this or that,—if he issue such demands, irrespective of their righteousness or wrongfulness,—if he require what he ought not, and what ought not to be complied with, then let the wife, in her great misfortune, look up to the God of the oppressed, and standing, like Vashti, in the mighty strength of virtue, decline obedience. In other words, let her obey God and her conscience, rather than man.

Esther.

Esther began to flourish about B. C. 462. She was a Jewess, resident in Susa, and daughter of Abihail, who appears to have been of the many among that people who declined returning to Canaan after the Babylonian captivity. Her parents having both died, she became the adopted daughter of her kinsman, Mordecai, who was one of the king's porters at his palace in Shushan, and who appears to have reared her up with extraordinary care. Esther is represented as possessing great beauty, and "obtained favor in the sight of all that looked upon her." She it was who, after the banishment of the virtuous Vashti from the king's presence, was selected by him to take her place, and received the royal crown at his hand. By her exaltation, she became the providential instrument of saving the people of her nation in the conspiracy for their destruction plotted by the infamous Haman. Greatly beloved by the king, he was ready to bestow upon her all her desire,—while thus signal advantages accrued to the Jewish people wherever scattered in that vast empire. Her elevation, and her triumph over Haman and all the enemies of her nation, are the capital incidents of her history, as given in the Scriptures. The number of years she lived, and whether the sequel of her history was equally prosperous as its commencement, are matters which are not reported to us.

Nor is it necessary. To act the part which she was commissioned to act, was glory sufficient for one princess, even if no further prosperity and happiness awaited her upon earth. The conspiracy of Haman, and its defeat, constitute one of the great and prominent events of Jewish history. Ahasuerus is king of the great Assyrian empire. Esther is his recently-wedded and beloved wife. Haman was the first of the nobility. Mordecai was one of the king's porters. Mordecai and Esther were Jews, and related to each other as above. He refuses to Haman the usual ceremonies of respect and reverence, paid to him by the other servants of the king. Whether Mordecai had sufficient reason for a course of conduct which placed in such imminent peril the existence of the whole Jewish people, is not related. Haman becomes greatly exasperated, and plots the ruin, not only of Mordecai, but of all his brethren throughout the empire. All arrangements are made for a simultaneous attack, and utter extermination. To this project of wholesale murder the king had given his consent, and had thus shown himself a fellow-murderer with his chief minister. The curses of posterity fall heavily upon the head of Haman in remembrance of this transaction. But if his name be so detestable, what shall be said of the man who, having power to prevent all the mischief, cordially consented to this greatest tragedy that was ever projected, and the successful execution of which would have covered with innocent blood the greatest empire on earth, and blotted from existence, in a single day, one of the nations of the world?

The human angel that was to step forth and turn away this most fatal storm, was the beautiful Esther. Instructed by Mordecai concerning the danger that was pending, and the part she was to act, she mediated with consummate address—brought into requisition all her great influence with her royal, brutal husband—procured the condemnation and execution of her nation's great enemy—obtained permission for the Jews in all the empire to stand upon their defense on the day appointed for their destruction,—and thus, by her timely agency, saved her kindred and people.

A high place is to be assigned to Esther, therefore, in the list of eminent women that have adorned this world. She did valiantly; nor can we wonder that her name should be so honored and dear in the minds of the Jewish people of every generation. Not only are we to contemplate her as eminent in intellectual ability, but as endowed also with extraordinary goodness of heart. The fate of her nation was hanging, for a time, upon her movements; and nobly did she fulfill the mission which the Divine providence had assigned to her. She laid her all upon the altar of the public welfare. "Fast ye for me," she saith to Mordecai and all the Jews; "I also and my maidens will fast likewise; and so will I go in unto the king, which is not according to the law; and if I perish, I perish." Such was the spirit and temper of the beloved Esther. She determined, if need be, to sacrifice herself for the safety of her kindred.

In the history of Esther there rises before us, with wonderful clearness and emphasis, one of those movements of special Providence which the pure mind discerns so constantly on the page of history. For aught that we can perceive, it was utterly irrespective of Esther's connection with the king that Haman receives the great offense which was likely to result so disastrously. We see not but the murderous and dreadful decree would have been made, whether she had ever beheld the king or not. Yet when it is made, and the frightful storm is gathering, she is directly there, and clothed, providentially, with an authority such as no other person upon earth could wield. When a fate the most disastrous and terrible of all their history was hanging over all that wide-spread people, the God of destinies had placed the one being of all others in the one position of all others, for the turning aside the dreadful blow! Such is the grand fact—the sublime development, in the inspired history of the illustrious Esther. We love her for the admirable qualities of her person. We respect her for the lofty place she was called to occupy. We profoundly venerate her for her accomplished tact and triumphant success in overthrowing a conspiracy the bloodiest, perhaps, and the most diabolical, in the annals of human history. At the same time, let us love, and venerate, and adore infinitely more the great unseen Hand that was concerned in all the phenomena of her history, and the Being who was himself the great actor amid these solemn movements. Verily, there is a God that sitteth in the heavens, who bringeth to naught the devices of wicked men, and into the pit which they prepare for others thrusts them down headlong to terrible destruction.

The daughter who may chance to read this brief essay will not, of course, infer that there are to be many instances such as that of Esther. Yet may every one be certain that, in the event of her full submission to the Divine hand, that hand shall accomplish in her, and by her, some good which may not be measured by earthly treasures.

The Virgin Mary.

MARY is the earliest of the female characters that meet us in the New Testament Scriptures; and she rises before us as the one of all the Bible whom, in the way of description or history, we approach the most reluctantly. We feel that though human, and inheriting "like passions" with her sex generally, yet, on the other hand, she stands out distinctly from all others, and that she is, as well in our thoughts, as in the angelic sallutation, "blessed among women." Special and profound reverence, therefore, shall be added to our sacred affection, as we glance at her who was divinely hailed as "highly favored,"—and who was the mother of Jesus.

Mary was the daughter of Heli, and was, as well as her husband, descended of the royal line of David. She appears to have been a native of Nazareth, and when she is first introduced by the sacred writer, her hand is pledged to Joseph, and the marriage-day is approaching. It is during this interesting interval that the great event of the Annunciation occurs. A solemn day was that in Mary's history—a day unexpected—unthought of previously—and afterwards never to be forgotten. Up to this morning she was as others of her sex and age, and bloomed, a lovely being, somewhere within the city of Nazareth. True, we know nothing of her previous history. Yet we do not think of her as having ever before looked upon superior beings, or listened, in amazement, to unearthly voices. There is no wonder, then, that when that angel being met her, she was astonished;—and that when those sentences of heavenly beauty fell upon her ear, she was troubled. No extraordinary destiny, it is probable, ever arose to occupy her youthful dreams. Her sober, thoughtful mind, as it gazed into the future, embraced, it is true, delightful prospects; yet were they such, and only such, as a thousand lovely maids have looked upon, as they welcomed the delicious visions of forthcoming and joyous happiness. Joseph, if we do not misjudge both him and her, was the man of all others to be greatly loved by Mary. Intelligent, righteous, candid, generous, and merciful, he was the fine and noble counterpart of that female loveliness and worth which, probably, have never been excelled. Her union with him was contemplated, then, with calm and sunny hope, and their united and happy destinies on earth would witness, as she trusted, a peaceful evening, and they would pass afterward away to the heavenly Canaan.

Were not something like the above the limits of Mary's modest, though brilliant hopes, on the morning of Gabriel's visit? But a scene new and altogether extraordinary opens now. The Virgin is no longer upon a level with others of her sex. "Blessed art thou among women," is announced to her from an authority more than human, and henceforth "all generations" must contemplate her as standing alone. There is none like her—there can be none. She is the first of her sex, from the ancient "mother of all living," down to the last maid that shall bloom in beauty at the opposite and far-off extremity of Adam's race. Standing as in the centre of human generations, there she rises, with a sublimity unearthly, to the gaze of a wondering world—her form beaming with a radiance soft, yet novel and awful, and with a beauty above human, and peerless. Whoever speaks of her now, let him pause as he pronounces a name not merely pleasant, but holy, and attaching to itself associations as interesting and as sublime as man's immortal weal. Is it a goddess as we approach her—a being once human and terrestrial, and now all suddenly deified, and registered with celestial intelligences? Nothing of this. Spare your adorations and your prayers. Worship God! Here rises no divinity. Humanity is still here; but who shall tell its exaltation? Who shall appreciate the overwhelming enchantment of this strange picture? The pen trembles and falls here. Amazement seizes the bewildered spectator;—the eye grows dim;—the spirit's depths are stirred;—the natural powers give way;—the whole being, like the Virgin alone and looking upon that angel stranger, is troubled;—strange visions, such as never waked before, rise up, though dimly—then flit away again, as within the shadows of eternity.

Who shall describe the interview, when that swift immortal hailed the gentle Mary? Who shall portray that presence? What was the beauty of that countenance?—the glory of that eye—the brilliancy of those tresses—the music of that voice—the divine gracefulness of those motions—the fragrance of those robes of immortality? Which way came he as he entered? In what direction lay his course as, retiring, he passed away heavenward ?

Is it wicked that, with longings irrepressible, we revolve such inquiries ? Since sometimes human eyes have looked upon heavenly forms, and human ears have listened to celestial voices, is it a forbidden curiosity when, in the soul's deep struggles, it looks out through the portals, and weeps to descry beings that once touched this earth—and have walked and conversed with humble and lowly ones—and in music such as is never heard from human lips, have whispered to one, "Thou art greatly beloved !" and to another, "The Lord is with thee !"

Thus was Mary saluted. Was she within doors, or abroad upon the mountain ramble ? Was it in open day, or when the shadows of night were reposing softly upon hill and vale ? Did he tarry long, or was he soon away again, nearing the shores of Paradise ? It is not essential ; nor is it essential that Gabriel should come to me. His mission to Mary was as if to every individual for whom a Saviour was about to be revealed.

It seems needless to remark the exceeding appropriateness of so sublime an announcement as that to the favored Mary. If mere men, as Isaac and the Baptist, eminent though they were, might be heralded by angel messengers, much more should we expect such extraordinary proclamation to precede the advent of Him who was the greatest of all prophets, and whose kingdom was to last forever. Strange that such a superhuman manifestation should ever raise a doubt in a Christian mind! What thoughtful man would not wonder, rather, at the absence of such species of notice? Is not the entire process of redemption superhuman? When the Divinity became united with humanity; when the rescue of a wicked world from sin, and from death eternal, was planned; when a greater work was about to be consummated on earth, than the creation of thousands of material worlds,—was it so strange that celestial messengers from heaven to earth should precede and accompany so momentous a crisis in God's providential and gracious dispensations? On the contrary, all is in keeping. It was fit that movements so sublime and wonderful should be announced by angels, and that voices from other worlds should be heard right early, proclaiming the coming of the Desire of all nations.

And the message is given—the maid listens with astonishment,—believes what she hears,—acquiesces in the Divine plans, and receives the angel's blessing.

When the scene again opens, Mary is hastening far from home to commune with Elisabeth. Arriving, strange salutations again meet her, as she enters the mansion of her cousin. Prophetic words are once more breathed forth, and again are the blessings of heaven pronounced upon the virgin, while, in glad response, her own lips are opened, and, in a song of matchless beauty, she praises the God who had exalted her to be the admiration of all generations.

The scene of her perplexity then follows soon; but Joseph is a just and feeling man, and his heart, though, doubtless, racked and torn with bitterest disappointment, yet leaned toward mercy. He would not destroy the supposed guilty one. He was prudent and sincere, and God met him and plead for the innocent, and banished all his fears, and restored him again to his virtuous and beloved Mary. "He will never suffer the righteous to be moved."

Jesus Christ is born!—"born of the Virgin Mary." Of this great event it scarcely becomes us to speak in this connection. It stands out prominently in the history of the universe, and will attract to itself the admiration of holy intelligences so long as "life and thought and being last." All suddenly it drew heaven down; and voices without number, and such as never before lighted on the ears of fallen beings, breathed their triumphant minstrelsy in the vicinity of this earth. Long before, indeed, the morning stars sang together, and all the sons of God shouted for joy. But this was when the world's foundations were laid, and before sin had spoiled the newly created scene. Four thousand years had rolled slowly and sadly away, while no heavenly harp was heard in human habitations, or abroad in blooming groves, or aloft in mid-air. Superior beings were away; or if, at distant intervals, they approached our world on errands of mercy or of vengeance, it was to linger but for a moment, and then again "fly swiftly" from scenes of guilt and woe too mournful for the eyes of angels. The moment of Christ's incarnation was the moment, in the history of man, when heavenly voices first sung in the ears of sinners. It was in the dark night, and shepherds, at their vigils, were the favored auditors. We wonder not that they were "sore afraid;" nor that, as they saw those hosts return heavenward, they said one to another, "Let us go to Bethlehem and see!"

Mary, as is natural, appears now and then, as we trace the inspired history of the Lord Jesus. Wherever we discern her, along his infancy and childhood, we always behold her deep and tender interest—her fullness of affection—her unfeigned modesty and humility—her sober thoughtfulness, and the exceeding propriety of her whole bearing and conduct. It might seem that, deeply penetrated with a sense of the transcendent dignity of her position, she most assiduously eschewed every word, and act, and thought, inconsistent with such elevation. She never obtrudes herself upon the popular gaze. Her words are few and select. Perfectly assured of the extraordinary character and destiny of her Son, she, at the same time, moves with the strictest prudence, and, instead of noise and ostentation, she "keeps all these things, and ponders them in her heart." In the public career of Christ, she is profoundly interested in all his movements—takes not her eye away from him —lingers near him to the last, and is in one of the groups which, standing afar off, sees him suspended from the cross. Then and there it was that she felt to the quick the wound predicted to her by Simeon, and a sword pierced through her own soul as she constrained herself to witness the agonies of Him who was, at the same time, her son and her Saviour. That son, (O, wonderfully beautiful!) in the very act of dying for the eternal life of a world, gave her in charge to the beloved disciple, in order that quietness and plenty might bless the evening of her days.

Elisabeth.

ELISABETH is a name of great reputation in the Holy Scriptures. She was of the daughters of Aaron, and wife of Zachariah, who was of the priesthood. The Scripture presentation of the character of these two persons is, that "they were both righteous before God, walking in all the commandments and ordinances of the Lord blameless." More than this, surely, need not be added. They were obviously not like thousands of their nation, and many even in the priesthood. They had not a mere outwardly righteousness, but a righteousness before God—a righteousness that was real, sincere, and such as met the Divine approval. It is highly refreshing, as well as interesting, to discern examples like these, moving amid that wicked generation. All accounts agree that the Jewish people had become strangely degenerate. Though they professed the worship of the true God, and the temple service was still maintained, yet were they an exceedingly rebellious and wicked people, and were rapidly filling up the measure of their iniquities. Many of the priesthood were among the vilest of men. They were full of hypocrisy, murder, debate, deceit, malignity, and almost every evil passion that was wont to riot in men abandoned to evil and wickedness. There seemed no epithet too dreadful for inspired lips to attach to them. They were blind guides, hypocrites—whited sepulchers—serpents, and vipers, and murderers. Even the members of the great council appear, almost to a man, to have been on a level with the very worst of men,—utterly regardless of justice, truth, or even decorum. And as it was with the higher classes, so was it with the multitude. Righteousness, goodness, and the fear of the Lord, seem to have almost utterly forsaken that favored people. They had received the law by the dispensation of angels, and had not kept it. Zachariah and Elisabeth, and others, here and there, stood out from this general mass of wickedness. They rose as pure and burning lights amid the darkness. The spirit of evil was all abroad; but they remained untainted, and held fast their integrity.

Such was Elisabeth. During many years of a wicked age, and encompassed by unrighteousness, she was righteous before God. She kept herself aloof from the raging flood of impiety. She joined her husband most fully and cordially in adhering to God and his law, amid surrounding darkness and violence. She looked for a brighter day, and departed not from the fear of God. Her house was a house of prayer. "The Scriptures" were there, and they were perused and regarded, and the law of God was laid up in her heart. We know of Elisabeth that she sincerely loved and worshiped the true God. She was pure in speech. She sanctified the Sabbath-day. She rendered to all their dues, and interfered with the rights of none. No one had reasonably any evil thing to say of her. She was blameless, harmless, without rebuke, before a wicked and perverse nation, among whom she shone as a pure and brilliant light.

How fit a companion was she for a priest of the most high God! How favored of Providence was Zachariah in the lovely companion of his life! And, on the other hand, how happy was such a one as Elisabeth, that she was joined with a man of prayer—a righteous man! What must have been the mutual influence, especially in that corrupt age, of their unflinching integrity, and unfailing righteousness! They joined hands for goodness and for heaven. They strengthened each other in the Lord their God. They were not unequally yoked together. Theirs was a marriage indeed—a union in the great things of God, and in the momentous interests of the soul.

God remembers his chosen ones, and often opens up before them new scenes of happiness, even in the present world. Continuing righteous before God, and walking regularly and constantly in His commandments and ordinances, it has more than once transpired that, after long years of trial, blessings as unexpected as they were valuable, have all suddenly been laid at the feet of the faithful ones. I have heard of a traveler who wandered long amid dark and apparently interminable forests. As he advanced, the dense thicket still arose before him, beyond which no field or sky arose on the weary eye ; and there seemed, as the sombre days and solitary nights passed slowly over him, only a deeper and deeper burial within the cold, damp wilderness. And yet he rallied fortitude and strength, and fanned the flickering flame of hope, and still advanced, until, as in a twinkling, a brilliant opening shone through the ancient forest-trees; and approaching, he looked in transport upon his long-desired and long-sought home, reposing in beauty amid the sunny vale beneath the eminence whereon he stood entranced. And then, as he looked up and breathed infinite gratitude into the ear of God, he forgot, in that hour of transport, all his dreary wanderings, and every dark anxiety and fear, and hailed his present happiness as an ample compensation from the Hand that doeth all things well.

Thus was it with Elisabeth. She, like Sarah of old, had passed into the vale of years, and without embracing a son,—an event which appears to have been counted a severe reproach and calamity by the ancient women. Yet mark what honor succeeds to such reproach—what prosperity triumphs over such calamity, in the examples of these illustrious worthies. Passing, both of them, beyond the line within which lie human hope and probability, mysterious beings are suddenly passing from heaven to earth,—and strange predictions are uttered, and new revelations astonish and cheer God's humble worshipers,—and renowned offspring, whose names are to be held in everlasting remembrance, rise before those "who were called barren." God's ways are a great deep, and His paths are not known.

A son is born to Elisabeth,—a son of rich and certain promise, and of sublime and glorious destiny. He was sacred from his birth, and the hand of the Lord was near him. He passed his childhood and youth away from public gaze; and as he grew in stature, his spirit waxed strong and mighty, and going in and out before his parents, they knew him to be ordered for extraordinary purposes.

Elisabeth's son became a prophet of the highest—the predicted Elijah of the New Testament dispensation—the forerunner of God's Messiah, turning multitudes to the Lord their God. He was great in the sight of the Lord—so great that none born of woman had been greater than he. True, he died disastrously, as have multitudes of others of whom the world was not worthy. Yet he finished his course, and passed early to take his place among the assembled prophets of former generations.

Daughter of Israel! How pure, as it flows to thee, is the voice of thine ancient sister! It whispers, "Be thou always sincerely and deeply righteous, nor be swerved from thy duty by one of all adverse influences. Hide the blessed law of God within thy heart, and let all thy private, domestic, and social walks be in exact accordance with its precepts. Join hands, in beauteous harmony, with thy husband, in all the ways of righteousness and holiness. If he is hastening up the path of life, hasten thou at his side. If he lingers, gently and cautiously direct his eye aloft, and, with thy soft hand, draw him onward. Love thou the house of God, and linger always near His altars. Count nothing unimportant which He has enjoined, and let all His ordinances be precious with thee. And be thou blameless—an Israelite indeed, in whom there is no guile. Thus God shall appear for thee; and brighter scenes shall yet open before thee—it may be in this life—certainly in the life to come."

Anna.

A FEW lines only of the Divine book are devoted to her; yet they tell of excellent things, and will bear the name of Anna, with honor, down to the latest generation of the Saviour's followers. On her first and only appearance upon the Divine page, she has traveled far down into the vale of years. The husband and companion of her youth was long since dead, and, resigning him to an early grave, it might seem that she had, at the same time, relinquished all earthly hopes—had consecrated herself to holy living—had dwelt long and earnestly amid the Scriptures, and had delighted to abide near the altar of God. The morning and evening service at the temple was dear to her; so also was the silent closet, and the prayer which went up from the heart to the Father who seeth in secret. Her soul was in sympathy with him of old, to whom the law of God was only delight, and in that law he meditated day and night. Long and intently had she pondered the ancient prophecies, and she saw that brighter days were laid up for her nation, and for the world. A prophetess herself, she held deep communings with holy men of old, and with them she inquired, and searched diligently concerning the great salvation which they prophesied. With them, was she intent upon what, or what manner of time, the spirit of Christ which was in them did signify, when it testified beforehand the sufferings of Christ and the glory that should follow. She saw that the fullness of time was come,—that Daniel's weeks were spent—and, as the watchmen waiting for the star of morning, she was looking. The Prince of Peace—the Messiah of God—the Desire of all nations—He whose kingdom was to absorb all other kingdoms, and was to last forever—the Redeemer of men;—toward this long predicted Being were directed the eyes of Anna the aged. Nor was she without kindred minds that, within that wicked city, were praying and expecting. In addition to the prophetic impulse which touched her own spirit, had she not conversed with the venerable Simeon, and heard him express his assurance of looking, before his death, upon the Lord's Anointed?

Interesting to the student of holy things are these hallowed openings through which we are permitted to look within the cloisters and the hearts of ancient godly ones. How unutterably refreshing, even to us, far distant spectators, to behold the spirit of prophecy again returning, after the long interval of hundreds of melancholy years! How welcome the renewed visits of ancient Gabriel—ancient, yet youthful, and glorious, and mighty, as when, long before, he flew, at God's command, and touched the beloved Daniel! O! how sublimely beautiful to hear heaven's voices breathing again through human organs! The songs of Zacharias, Simeon and Anna, joined with those angel responses high up above the enchanted shepherds, breathe forth a chorus whose swift echoings along this dying world have startled millions into life—entranced them as they passed on through their pilgrimage—while, lying down to die at last, they still turned to listen to the great anthem of salvation as they "breathed their lives out sweetly there!"

And who might adequately measure the transports of the aged Anna? During many, many years, she had seen "through a glass darkly." True, she had hope of the promise made of God unto the fathers; unto which promise, instantly serving God, day and night, she hoped to come. She looked to see the promised Seed before her death. She longed that the clearer light should shine and that "the glory of Israel" might rise, for once, upon her eyes, ere her weary frame should sink into the dust.

She was heard. At the exact moment, the venerable Simeon "came, by the Spirit, into the temple;" and Anna was seen "coming in that instant." There they stood, on that remembered day, and as if representative of all men and women. There they both looked upon the Messiah,—both rejoiced with joy unspeakable,—both gave the prophetic testimony of his coming,—and both sent their praises, a sweet savor, up to the eternal throne.

Nor could this suffice for the enraptured Anna. See her, as she passes from house to house, and from street to street, seeking out the praying, hoping ones, assuring them that the Redeemer had come. Pure and brilliant is that light to those witnessing its last shining. That aged voice grows young again; that withered countenance beams with unwonted radiance; that faded eye grows bright with celestial fire. New and strange energy pervades that tottering frame. She takes hold of strength—pushes diligently her final effort—and departed not till she spake of Him to all that looked for redemption in Jerusalem.

Ye aged mothers in spiritual Israel! Weep not, for your light is come, and the glory of the Lord is risen upon you! The world, it is true, grows dim, and those that look out of the windows are darkened, and the doors are shut in the streets, and the daughters of music are brought low, and fears are in the way, and the grasshopper is a burden. As the trembling autumn leaf, ye are ready to drop and be unseen. Yet cling to the Hope of "the holy women in the old time, who trusted in God." Continue in supplications and prayers, as the closing days and nights pass heavily, perhaps painfully, away. Memory declines; yet seize upon a few exceeding great and precious promises, or upon only *one*, if sometimes all others fade from view. Flesh and heart fail; yet lean, with unyielding confidence, upon Him who is the strength of your hearts, and your portion forever. The speech is feeble and slow; yet use it to praise God, and give him perpetual thanksgiving. Pronounce often the name of your Redeemer, and speak of Him "to all that look for redemption." Be not in haste to say that the days of your usefulness are gone. No marvel if your evening sun shall go down in the midst of life's great harvest-time! At all events, prophesy while you may—praise while you live! Still sweep the broken, tuneless instrument, till the glad day of its exchange for the harp of eternity!

"I'll praise Him while He lends me breath,
And, when my voice is lost in death,
Praise shall employ my nobler powers;
My days of praise shall ne'er be past,
While life, and thought, and being last,
Or immortality endures."

The Woman of Samaria.

There seems an air of mystery accompanying this woman. Was she, or was she not, a woman of virtue? Against the favorable hypothesis, there stands the declaration, that when Christ conversed with her she had had five husbands, and was then in possession of a man who was not her husband. Nothing else appears in the narrative prejudicial to her reputation; while, on the contrary, the whole presentation, with the above exception, exhibits her under favorable aspects. What then of the exception?

That she had had five husbands, is no conclusive evidence against her; for so many might have died early, and with no blame on her part. Or some of them might have separated themselves from her by divorce, in accordance with a custom so painfully prevalent at that time, both with Samaritans and Jews. The darkest shade appears, therefore, when Christ reminds her that the one whom she now had was not her husband. But criminality is uncertain even yet: for the person alluded to may have been a husband only in prospect, and not actually such at the time of the conversation; so that with exact propriety, and, also, consistently with her virtue, the Lord might have said to her, "He whom thou now hast is not thy husband." All this, we repeat, may have been, while yet, we are obliged to admit that, so far as the language quoted is concerned, there is reason for unpleasant doubt. We may say, however, that the conversation, as a whole, inclines us to the favorable decision.

For, first, unless the sentence of Christ just quoted be regarded as such, he seems to utter to the Samaritan woman no reproof for immorality. All his other observations to her appear to be such as he might have very properly addressed to any virtuous and intelligent woman of Samaria. Then again, on the hypothesis of her criminality, every one has wondered at the turn of her thoughts on becoming convinced that Christ was a prophet. If he has just convicted her of disgraceful conduct, and convinced her of his knowledge of her character, how did it happen that she, as her first thought, pounced upon the long-disputed question of the Jews and Samaritans, touching the appropriate place of worship? Supposing her innocence, her immediate inquiry on this subject was perfectly natural. Now seemed to her a highly favorable opportunity to gain an inspired decision of this long-contested matter. But supposing her guilt, all this train of thinking and conversation looks unnatural and strained. She stands, on this hypothesis, a convicted harlot, before one whom she judged a prophet of God. Under such circumstances, would there be any disposition—any tendency, to revert to the question as to where men ought to worship? What has she to do with worship? Or what cares she for the fathers, or the mountain, or place where they praised the God of Israel? If, after such conviction of her guilt as is here supposed, she utters anything more, will there be no apology—not a single accent of penitence? Will she still proceed in conversation, precisely as though her position in society is without reproach? And where also is the reproof from Christ, which would seem to have been due to a woman thus convicted of sin? How is it—she being guilty—that he still converses with her as a woman of purity as well as of judgment, and discourses to her of the true and spiritual worship about to be introduced? When, on another occasion, a woman was arraigned before him as guilty of adultery, he charged her to sin no more. Why was there not a similar charge, if she were a similar character, to the woman of Samaria? Was it meet for the Saviour of the world to hold high converse with a woman of ill-fame, touching subjects in which we cannot conceive she would feel any interest? "Repent of this thy wickedness," would seem a far more pertinent address.

Yet again, this woman is obviously looking for the Messiah. She knows that he is coming, and she is expecting him soon. At the same time, such is her confidence in him, that she is assured he will teach her everything necessary. All this sounds like an upright and well-informed woman of Samaria; but it is difficult to predicate such sentiments of an adulteress; and equally incongruous, under such circumstances, is the Lord's profession of Messiahship. To this woman he tells—even before he has told any other person—that he was the Christ; while, upon the unfavorable hypothesis, he makes this very important revelation to a bad woman, and one exercising no penitence or prayer. All this may have been, but it is certainly unaccountable.

We may look a step further. On hearing that the Being who talked with her was the Messiah, and confiding in what she heard, she hastens into the city; and as she communicates the intelligence, and tells the ground of her confidence, "many of the Samaritans of that city believed on him for the saying of the woman." What! when this same woman was of ill repute—whose good name and character were gone? Why this high degree of confidence in a wicked woman, so that her proclamation of the Messiah was at once received implicitly by a multitude? And why were so many others ready to go, at her word, and see for themselves the wondrous manifestation?

From all these considerations, there appears much reason to conclude that the woman of Samaria, with whom the Lord Jesus held one of his most important conversations recorded in the sacred book, bore not that disreputable character which many are accustomed to ascribe to her. One single expression of Christ seems to throw her into suspicion; but that expression may admit of a construction favorable to the one addressed; while, with the supposition of her innocence, the whole conversation and narrative are harmonious, but with the supposition of her guilt, there occur decided incongruities.

We prefer, therefore, as well for the sake of truth, as for the sake of the memory of the Samaritan woman, to count her as being a woman of unstained reputation—as having passed through vicissitudes of life which, though extremely uncommon in Christian society, were yet far less singular as growing out of known customs of the people of that nation and age. To have been joined to five husbands, and to be contemplating a union with a sixth, would obviously be deemed reproachful under Christian light; it all might have been entirely innocent in Samaria, and even in Judea, before the voice of Christ re-established the true regimen touching marriage and divorce.

At the same time, all parties will be profoundly interested in the scene at Jacob's well. There sat Christ the Lord, wearied with his journey—and it was high noon—and the powerful sunbeams, falling upon him, had increased his weariness and excited his thirst. His disciples, meanwhile, were gone to the neighboring city for provisions, and Jesus was alone when "the woman" made her appearance. The dialogue that ensues is surprisingly rich in spiritual instruction, and marked throughout with what may be termed the most perfect naturalness and simplicity. There is seen the transition, as beautiful as it is natural, from the cool and refreshing waters of that well, to the living water which Christ bestows, and whereof, if a man drink, he shall thirst no more. The grace he gives shall satisfy, with perfect happiness, the soul that receives it—waking within him perpetual delights, and causing to spring up, as an unfailing fountain, a bliss full, all-sufficient, glorious, eternal. And in the midst of this interview and conversation arises also the most welcome assurance, that the Almighty source of happiness is to be confined to no one city or mountain. The veil of the temple is about to be rent in twain from the top to the bottom, and the way into the holiest of all is to be made accessible to all of every nation and place—while he will seek such to worship him, as worship in spirit and in truth.

The woman of Samaria retires from the presence of Christ a believer in him as the Saviour of the world; and as she tells the story of her conversion, many others receive the same faith, and are saved in like manner. Forget not this one suggestion, daughters of Zion! This woman had found Christ, and she would not have done well to hold her peace. Straight was the path she took, as, forgetful of her pitcher, she hasted away to the city. "Come!" was her earnest word;—"Come, see the Messiah!" Too great was the blessing she had found, to be concealed for a moment. And as she told the story of her faith, many others believed also. Thus shall it ever be. This simple and sincere testimony, on the lips of the Christian, shall be powerful in its influence, and many shall hear, and fear, and turn to the Lord. It is a mournful feature of Christian society in these days, that what is termed common conversation strongly tends to be worldly rather than spiritual. Religion is too much confined to churches, and sermons, and prayers. It flows not forth, as it ought, to mingle itself with all the affairs of life, and to sanctify all the minutiæ of our transient existence upon earth. We would not advocate a noisy or ostentatious religion. Christians must of course, be wise, as well as holy. But we would welcome the day when the spiritual element shall enter more freely and fully into our daily intercourse and conduct;—when the glory of God shall be in our eye, even in the matters of eating and drinking; and when no corrupt communication shall proceed from our mouths, but such as is good to the use of edifying, that it may, like that of the Samaritan woman, minister grace to the hearers.

The Woman of the bloody issue.

HERE rises another illustrious instance of woman's faith. The person concerned had been long an invalid, and her disorder was of a highly distressing and discouraging character. Twelve melancholy years had passed over her since the commencement of her infirmity; one and another physician had prescribed for her; many remedies had been proposed and tested. Sometimes hope would animate her; then again failure and discouragement would ensue. In many instances harsh measures had been adopted, subjecting her to much distress and anguish. All this she could gladly have endured, if, beyond her sufferings, she could have welcomed returning health and happiness. But every experiment, however painful, was without effect, save to leave her in a more distressed and hopeless condition than before. Meanwhile, so desirable to her was the great blessing of health, she had spent all her substance in purchasing those vain and injurious medicaments. She had sold all that she had, to purchase the healing of her infirmity; and when all was gone she was "nothing better, but rather grew worse." Her sickness remained with her when her means of sustenance were gone, and no house remained to shelter her—nor wardrobe from which to clothe and warm her sinking frame.

It was under these dark circumstances that she "heard of Jesus." His fame was now spread abroad. Vast multitudes from various quarters had flocked to see him, when they had heard what great things he did. Many sick and diseased people had been all suddenly restored to health. Distressed and dying ones had been borne to him from various regions, and, in every case, they rose up at his command, and returned home with the fair bloom of perfect health sitting upon their countenances. Raging demoniacs had been released from the destroyer, and were sitting among their friends, clothed, and in their right mind. Hapless lepers, at his touch, had felt their flesh renewed, in a twinkling, as the flesh of a little child, and went from his presence publishing abroad the great things that Jesus had done for them.

Of all this, and more than this, she of whom we write did hear, and, as she heard, she seized upon faith for her own recovery. She had gone down to deep extremity. Her health, and home, and bread were all gone. Her last hope seemed to be dying, when came the tidings of the heavenly Physician.

From this moment she seems to us to have entertained no lurking doubt. She saw that her time had now come; that, after long sorrow, the hour of joy was at hand; and the mournful night that had so long hung over her, was about to end in a bright and glorious morning.

We may readily imagine that she made no delay in hastening to Christ. Her faith was unusual, and it bore her swiftly to where the multitude were assembled, and urged her, as with a determined and final effort, through the crowds that surrounded and thronged the Messiah. Who may tell her emotions at this moment of her history, and as, in her violence, she said within herself, "If I may but touch his clothes, I shall be whole!" What then was the trembling energy of that frail hand, as she thrust it forth to realize the blessed contact! She touched; and according to her faith so it was done to her. Her plague was healed straightway, and she felt the tide of health at once flowing blissfully through her long-wearied and sickly frame. "Who touched my clothes?" And as she heard these words, and his eye fell upon her, she feared exceedingly. For a moment it seemed, perhaps, that her Saviour was displeased with the liberty she had taken—was about to rebuke her forwardness—and resume the virtue that, without being asked for, had "gone out of him." An awful moment must that have been to the trembling woman. How could she lose again the priceless blessing which she had just received? And how could she endure, in addition, the reproach of the great Deliverer? It seemed a great and momentous crisis, and she is speedily prostrated before him. Here she tells him all; and, in return, there is no rebuke. The accents of infinite beauty and love fall upon her ear, saying, "Daughter, thy faith hath made thee whole—go in peace, and be whole of thy plague." His sacred approbation and assurance are given now, and the reward of her faith is pleasant, as are the months and years of joyous health and sunny peace, after long periods of suffering and discouragement.

The faith of this woman stands among the most precious and remarkable examples. It was a confidence in the infinite exuberance of the Messiah's power and goodness. In her eye he was an inexhaustible fountain of glory and virtue. In him she saw in realization the vision of the prophet, and the very clothing of Jesus was the robes of salvation, and the smell of his garments was as the smell of Lebanon. In her mind it was safety to be near him, and health and life to hear his voice. She beheld in Christ the infinite fullness that was ever ready to burst forth, and like the electric spark, to fly wherever a connecting medium, slight though it were, might be established. The putting forth of her hand to touch the sacred vestments, was but the visible emblem of her struggling and confiding soul. Her spirit leaned, without the slightest hesitation, upon the Spirit Almighty and All-benevolent, and was of course not disappointed.

Blessed are they whose faith in Christ's power and mercy is unlimited, and who always and joyfully realize that he is able to save to the uttermost!

Mary of Bethany.

PASSING out of St. Stephen's gate, in the eastern wall of the city of Jerusalem, crossing the brook Cedron, and passing near the garden of Gethsemane, then turning, and, with the brook on your right, following its southerly course a little space, and presently circling eastward up Mount Olivet, and crossing a double ridge, you descend into a deep and narrow vale, about two miles from the city you have just left. Here is *Bethany*,—so famous in the evangelical narrative, and wreathing with its name associations—some, beautiful as the walks of angels—others, awful as the voices from the spirit world. Here was one of the favorite resting-places where the Saviour of the world resorted for refreshment and repose, and here were mansions where He was often welcomed who came to be for salvation to the ends of the earth.

It was in one of these happy homes where bloomed in modest beauty Mary of Bethany—one of the purest and loveliest characters of the Holy Scriptures, and answering, almost without exception, the true idea of female exellence. Martha was her sister, and Lazarus her brother, while the parents of the three were probably no longer among the living. Several circumstances seem to bespeak the more than ordinary respectability of this interesting family. That they were above want, is a likely inference from their frequent and generous hospitalities toward Christ and his companions, as also from the expensive anointing, by Mary, at the feast of Simon;—while their respectability, as well as wealth, is an idea harmonious with the attention and sympathy exhibited to the sisters in the visits of condolence from Jerusalem after the death of their brother.*

There belongs, however, to Mary a character infinitely more valuable than what might arise from worldly riches and reputation. Her earliest appearance in the inspired narrative is one of exceeding interest. She is listening with profound attention and reverence to the great Teacher who has condescended to honor her residence with his presence, and speak to that circle, of matters the most interesting to them in the universe. Mary especially drinks in the words of life. All things else appear to lose their hold upon her attention and affections. The outward world has lost its attractions, and loved associates are, for the time, neglected and forgotten. Even the domestic arrangements are esteemed of no importance in com-

* Dr. Olin.

parison of the words that flow, as spirit and life, to her soul. She forgets her customary share of the household duties, while the more careful Martha is left to serve alone. She has found meat to eat such as the world knows not of. A scene of enchantment has opened before her vision, and she would fain gaze upon it forever. To tear herself away from the Redeemer's feet, and cease to listen to his voice, is as if passing from the charms of the heavenly paradise to roam amid the rough hills and ravines around her earthly abode. A glimpse of the immortal life is affecting deeply the heart of Mary. What is the world to her,—"its pomp, its pleasure, and its nonsense all?" What is there here save emptiness? On what shall she lay her hand, and say, "See, this is abiding and permanent?" Whither shall she run, and entering, exclaim, "Lo, this is my fortress and my strong tower?" In what fragrant and peaceful bowers shall she recline, and, reposing there, sing, "Here be my rest forever?" On what peaceful shore shall she stand, and, amid the thrilling of unutterable happiness, whisper to herself, "Here glides the river of the water of life?" On what countenance of entrancing loveliness shall she look, whose spiritual beauty, and whose smiles divine, shall still enrapture, when the stars shall have long since set behind the shadows of eternity? "Mary, come to my help, that I serve not alone!" "Martha, entreat me not to leave His feet, from whose lips are flowing the words of eternal life!"

"Master, bid her that she help me!"

"Martha,—Martha! thou art troubled about many things. One thing is needful: and Mary hath chosen that good part, which shall never be taken away from her."

But sadness came at length, and entered the once pleasant mansion of Martha and Mary. Their dear and only brother was sick, and it was a sickness unto death. As he declined from day to day, and all human help and wisdom proved abortive, it was natural that they should think of the great Physician who had healed so many of their sicknesses. He was away beyond the Jordan; yet a messenger is suddenly despatched with the intelligence that the one whom he loved was sick. Jesus delays his visit, and for the present withholds his power, and the brother beloved is left to die. Four days after his burial, Christ and his disciples arrived in the vicinity, and Martha hastens to meet him. The more quiet Mary waits, at the house, the Saviour's coming, or tarries till she is bidden to approach his presence. She comes with the same salutation which Martha used, deeply expressive at once of their faith and their sorrow. "Lord, if thou hadst been here, my brother had not died!" Thus spake Mary, as, low at his sacred feet, she wept in her bitterness. Here ceased her words, but more eloquent still was the agony of her grief. The Lord was silent. She especially was dear to Christ, and as he saw the intensity of her mourning, his own spirit groaned and wept.

Great and awful was the transaction of that day at the grave of Lazarus. There stood the twelve. They had often seen the brother of Martha and Mary, and had been partakers of his cheerful hospitalities. "Our friend Lazarus," were the pleasant words by which the Lord had spoken of him when they heard of his illness. There stood also the visitors from Jerusalem, who had come to Bethany, that day, on a visit of condolence and sympathy. And there were the two sisters—their hearts swollen with grief too great to be comforted. Lastly, there stood the weeping Son of God—weeping with them that wept—mingling his sacred tears with those of the bereaved. And there, at the same time, He stood girded with omnipotence, while, as he spake, the reverberations of that voice rolled through paradise. The time had come when the dead heard the voice of the Son of God and lived. A slight tumult is heard, for a moment, from within that dark and noisome cavern, while without, all eyes have ceased to weep, and are gazing with trembling amazement toward the aperture. He is coming, —Heaven pity us! The vestments of death are upon him, and his swathed face is pale and thin; but his eyes are open, and the fire of life is again there. "Loose him, and let him go!"

After that, Mary could never for a moment forget the great Deliverer. She loved him before, and was never happier than when sitting at his feet, and hearing his word. But now, added to all his other unspeakable benefits, he had restored her dear and only brother, and had lighted up her desolated home with unbounded rejoicing.

The anointing succeeds in the house of Simon, as Jesus was sitting at his table in company with Lazarus and others. The ointment was of great price, and as Mary poured it upon the sacred person of the Messiah, he testified of her that she did it for his burial. Whether she had received directly from his lips or otherwise the impression that he was soon to die, is not revealed, though highly probable. She would perform this last kind office for him, and as her ministries must so shortly cease, she would spare no expense in whatever service might be proper or agreeable. Injurious reproaches fall upon her for her apparent profusion and waste; yet the greatest of advocates pleads in her behalf, and promises that her deed should be told for a memorial of her as far and as long as his blessed Gospel should be preached.

Martha.

"Now Jesus loved Martha." She, as well as her sister Mary, had a select place in the heart of Him who knew all men; and hence, we may safely infer for Martha a pure and excellent character. One of her prominent features appears to have been that of hospitality. Her house at Bethany was, as we have seen, one of the special resting-places of Christ and the apostles. Like the woman of Shunem, she prepared the place of lodging, in order that holy ones, at their pleasure, might turn in thither. A thousand families, and a thousand sunny houses there were, where Jesus and his companions never entered. They "knew him not." He came to his own, but his own received him not—neither into their hearts, nor into their circles. But blessed were those doors that opened as he approached, and the roofs that often sheltered the one who had not where to lay his head. Such was the house of Martha. To the "Man of sorrows" that was one of his dearest homes amid his earthly sojournings. There he was ever welcome. Smiles of friendship always greeted him as he entered. Holy sympathy burned there, while coldness and hostility full often met him elsewhere. None arose with more alacrity than Martha to provide for the refreshment of the Saviour. None was more careful than she that every arrangement for his entertainment and comfort should be correspondent with her views of his lofty dignity and transcendent worth. Too much could not be done—too many hands could not be employed—viands too many, or too delicious, could not be provided for Him who came to save the lost. True, we once hear from his lips a gentle reproof of her exuberant preparations, and her excessive solicitude, cautioning her to remember that her care about transient comforts should not be allowed to interfere with that higher and eternal festival which he came to provide.

A deeply interesting passage in Martha's history is her interview with Christ on his tardy arrival after the death and burial of her brother. Martha, with her sister, had communicated the tidings of his illness,—and their message, on this occasion, was as affecting as it was modest and beautiful. "Lord, behold he whom thou lovest is sick," were the words of their brief epistle,—brief, for all attention was requisite for the help of their dying brother; dutiful, that brother was greatly beloved by the Saviour; unassuming, they would not venture to invite his attendance, though their wishes are deeply and strongly intimated. "Whom thou lovest;"—may not his special affection possibly induce him to be present with his healing mercy? Yet he hastens not to come, and Lazarus sleeps and is buried. At length Jesus arrives in the vicinity, and Martha, with her characteristic ardor, goes forth to meet him. Many visitors from Jerusalem were there to sympathize with the sorrowful sisters; yet vain, in that dark hour, was all human consolation; while, that from Jesus she still looked for some relief, there can be but little doubt. At all events, she will hasten, and pour out her sorrows before him. She believed him to be good beyond all others—who knows but he may help and relieve though in ways unknown?

Something like this may be supposed to have

been Martha's mind, as she met the Saviour, and, in her deep agony, exclaimed: "Lord, if thou hadst been here, my brother had not died." Blessed was her confidence, so far as it went, in the power of the Messiah. Yet it should have reached further. Christ could heal, whether near or far away. But pity thou her distress, and forget the confusion it may have induced, and overlook also the seemingly implied reproach upon the Lord for the delay that looked so fatal! Courage and faith are in the ascendant, as she adds, "But I know that even now, whatever thou wilt ask of God, he will give it thee." Martha is evidently venturing her eye upon the restoration of her lost brother. A broad and startling hint is here thrown out, of a secret hope which she does not plainly utter. A prayer of his would prevail greatly, if it could be that he should be disposed to "ask of God." Martha's faith here was mighty, not perfect. The Son had "life in himself," as well as the Father; and he will lead her higher. "Thy brother shall rise again," he answered; and as he spoke, it was with the authority of omnipotence, and he meant that the rising would be immediate. Martha is still confused, as well as sad, and falling back upon the long-admitted fact of a final resurrection,—"I know," she saith, "that he shall rise again at the resurrection at the last day." There the Saviour meets her—the finisher of her faith: "I am the resurrection and the life!" Full conviction flashed now upon Martha.

She saw that the raising of the dead was the prerogative of Christ—whether at the final day, or at present—a new hope kindled within her heart, and, at the intimation of Jesus, she hastened to call her sister.

Christ is near the tomb, and orders the stone, closing up the entrance, to be removed. At this moment of overwhelming excitement, Martha's courage fails, and her eye transiently reverts from life to death, and *sight* instead of *faith*, for a moment, predominates. A gentle reproof meets her from the voice that is about to call the dead to life,—and then the great crisis occurs, and Lazarus lives again on earth.

Martha and Mary.

HAVING glanced separately at Martha and Mary, it may not be amiss to view them briefly together, and as they stand related to each other. The Bible student who carefully ponders these two "elect ladies," will not fail to become more and more interested in the contemplation. He will see them possessing common features of character, and such a kind of similarity as might be expected to exist in two sisters reared up together, and coming constantly in contact with like associations and influences. He will, at the same time, discern a distinction—a distinction so permanent and marked as to entitle them to be considered as representatives of two important classes of the sex, neither of which alone would meet the wants of society, and standing as, in a sense, complements to each other.

Among the qualities that were common to the two sisters, we easily discern that of *intelligence.* They were, both of them, women of mind; and were, doubtless, respectable for their general acquirements and information. They were well read in the Jewish Scriptures, and their circumstances of competence, and the position they appear to have held in society, indicate that, in respect to intellectual attainments, they were inferior to few of their sex in the circles where they moved. Martha's interesting colloquies with Christ just previous to her brother's resurrection, clearly evince her intelligence, regarded as a Jewess. She had studied and digested the doctrines and teachings of the Jewish Scriptures, while her views had received ample enlargement and elevation from her intercourse with the great Teacher. Equally discernible, though in a different way, is the intelligence of Mary. She, as well as Martha, had given attention to sacred things—had been conversant with the Scripture prophecies, and seemed even more intent than her sister upon learning of Him who was meek and lowly in heart, and who yet knew all things. On one occasion, at least, Mary's extraordinary diligence in hearing the instructions of Christ, was esteemed by her sister as interfering with those domestic interests and duties in which they were accustomed cordially to participate.

Again, these sisters cherished a *common faith.* They were both believers in the ancient Scriptures, and both of them most cordially welcomed Christ as the promised Messiah. Martha did but speak the deep sentiment of herself and her sister when she uttered to Christ that distinct and beautiful confession, saying, "I believe that thou art the Christ, the Son of God, which should come into the world." With such a confession as this, their whole conduct was delightfully harmonious. They never appeared to doubt, for a moment, that Jesus was the Christ, the Saviour of the world. As such they received him and his companions to their cheerful hospitalities;—as such they sat at his feet, and heard his words,—and beckoned him to come to them in trouble,—and leaned upon his power, as upon no merely human help,—and saw in him fully and literally revealed the resurrection and the life.

Thus they possessed a *common piety.* Both of them feared and loved God, and were ardently attached to him whom they firmly believed to be the great and promised Messiah. Their love to Christ, it is true, went out under different modes of manifestation; yet was it, perhaps, equal in strength and constancy in those two hearts, and if with unequal speed, yet with equal certainty, would they have embraced the stake for the sake of Him whom their souls loved.

A *common hospitality* was also theirs. Equally rejoiced were they to receive Christ and his apostles within their mansion at Bethany. Their smiles of joy were harmonious, as they embraced the privilege of ministering to their necessities. Nothing in the eye of Martha was too good—no domestic service was too great, if it were for the comfort of her illustrious guest, and his favored disciples. So felt also the gentle Mary. Her hospitality was equal to Martha's, though modified at times, in its manifestations, by other preponderating sentiments hereafter to be noticed. If Martha flew to spread plenteously her table, Mary rejoiced in her sister's zeal, though that zeal might, now and then, reproach her own apparent deficiency or neglect. Their varying movements in the presence of their guests meant not that within those two noble hearts there dwelt not a harmony of cordiality, but they indicated a difference rather with which those hearts cherished other views, and other motives of conduct. Both were alike hospitable—one, from another and a lofty influence, was less attentive to the conduct which hospitality might suggest.

But passing from these and other instances of resemblance, it is time to notice those very obvious points of distinction and difference between these interesting sisters.

Thus Martha was marked by more than ordinary activity both of body and mind. She was quick of perception—vivid and strong in her views of external propriety—and of great promptness in action. Her eye, ever active and direct, appreciated with a glance the outward, the visible, the decorous. She lacked not a strong mind and a good heart,—yet she was, at the same time, solicitous that all arrangements with which she was concerned should be orderly and becoming. We may easily guess that her house, in all its apartments and furniture, was well-ordered, neat, and inviting. There was a tendency in her to be disturbed at the sight of anything deranged or untasteful. She loved to hear the words of Christ; yet she loved again to minister to his wants—to provide every physical comfort, and was careful to omit no attentions of this sort that her nice discernment saw to be becoming, or her means allowed her to furnish. In contemplating her, we fail not to be strongly reminded of the wise man's masterly portraiture of the virtuous woman, whose price is far above rubies: "She looked well to the ways of her household, and ate not the bread of idleness."

Mary, on the other hand, was more thoughtful than she was energetic and animated. She was meditative rather than active. The outward and the noisy had less attractions for her, and commanded less of her attention and care. If she might converse with the Lord Jesus, and listen to his heavenly wisdom, all else seemed to her as comparatively of no account. She could easily forget the little activities due to order, and even to hospitality, while she would lose herself amid the charms of sacred and holy visions. In her raptures with the divine, she tended to forget the human. Tasting the meat that endureth to everlasting life, it almost escaped her thoughts that even the food that perishes is for a time necessary. Her eye on the part which shall never be taken away, she seemed exposed to utter disregard of that action which, though immediately directed to temporal consequences, was yet as capable of being performed to the glory of God, as even those exercises that are of a more spiritual and more elevated order.

Martha, again, was *forward*;—yet not in that sense which is deemed indecorous and offensive. She was forward to speak; and if, at times, her words were hasty, yet were they in general judicious as well as pleasing. She was forward to move; yet hers were the movements of benevolence and generous sentiment. Her hands longed to be occupied with some affectionate acts, such as might conduce to the comfort and happiness of worthy ones. In her graceful forwardness, she could not do enough for her Saviour and his followers. Her step was as elastic as it was joyous; her movements were as sprightly as they were efficient, whenever she might administer to the necessities of those who were despised and rejected by many, even of her own friends and associates. Martha was forward; yet was it a forwardness with which we could not dispense in the female sex. It wakes a thousand streams of blessedness; it soothes a thousand sorrows; and wipes multitudes of tears away. It flies where the weary and the faltering are; its voice is as exhilarating as it is prompt and musical. It is, in a word, one of the capital charms of the female character; which being abstracted from the sex, one half the brilliancy and beauty of human society would be, at once, extinguished forever.

Mary was more remarkable for her retiredness; a quality, by the way, by no means inconsistent with becoming forwardness; while the two have been often blended, with exceeding loveliness, in the same individual. It was easy for Mary to exchange the bustle of business, and the excitement of conversation, for some obscure place at Jesus' feet. She loved the Saviour as well as Martha; yet while Martha goes out promptly to hail him as he approaches the mourning family, Mary sits still in the house. Martha proceeds without ceremony, and as soon as she hears his coming; Mary waits till the Master calls for her. She sought to linger in seclusion from the view of the multitude, leaving each more prominent and public duty to the management of her stronger and more active sister. Mary was the delicate and pure lily blooming in the vale; her sister was the brilliant rose, opening itself freely to the broad sunbeams.

Martha, yet again, was *social.* Prompt to move and act, she was equally ready to speak.

She was eminently a communicative being. Her buoyant and artless mind delighted to unburden itself to a friend. If within her mind were thoughts, whether of complaint or of congratulation—whether hopeful or fearful, they were wont to leap forth to meet the mind of an associate. And if, at times, and from reasons already alluded to, her words seemed verging toward impatience, or even severity, yet may we safely infer that the general character of her sociality was in harmony with her intelligent mind, and her generous and noble heart. Kind words—elevated, sprightly, and pure words, were those that fell more usually from the lips of Martha. Her conversation, doubtless, constituted one of the prominent attractions presented by her house to the Saviour and his apostles. And, after disputing in the temple with the perverse and stupid Jews, it was with genuine gratification, both to himself and to his companions, that he retired at evening to Bethany, and there, with spirits purer and more congenial, held high and heavenly converse. Nor can we forbear the impression, that in these delightful colloquies, Martha, on the part of her family, bore a prominent part.

For of the words and conversation of Lazarus, nothing, I believe, is reported; and Mary, as is obvious, while she was swift to hear, was slow to speak. She seems a listener, rather than as a sharer in the conversations that are passing. One of the strokes of the evangelic pen characterizing the beloved Mary was, that she "sat at Jesus' feet, and heard his word." She was a hearer, and was not careful to speak. Like another Mary of whom we read, she appeared disposed, rather, to "keep all these things, and ponder them in her heart." She speaks, indeed, at times. Her grief, for instance, breaks forth in words, on meeting Jesus near the tomb of her brother—"My brother had not died!" But there she pauses, and tears flow instead of words. She does not, like Martha, proceed to express any faith for the future, and thus draw forth the Saviour into conversation. Martha and her Lord had just exchanged sentiments of the greatest interest, and that in a dialogue commenced by Martha. When he meets Mary, no colloquy ensues. He listens to her mournful reflection touching his absence. He witnesses the gushing flood that followed her few struggling words, and weeps with her.

Finally, Martha was *solicitous*. A fullness of faith cannot be claimed for her; at least previous to her last-recorded conversation with the Lord Jesus. Her temperature was ardent; her discernment of the appropriate and the true was vivid; her motions of mind and body were rapid and earnest. Hence, an unruffled and undisturbed spirit was not naturally so facile an attainment with her as with others of a different constitution.

And of a different constitution was her sister Mary. Hence, in part, her superior quietness. If Martha was sometimes careful and troubled about many things, Mary often failed to sympathize in her sister's solicitudes. Nor, in her quietness, was she careful to answer the reproof of Martha, as the latter complained to Jesus of her seeming negligence. There appears, likewise, the same indifference when, in connection with the anointing at Simon's feast, she was accused of wastefulness. In all instances she wears the same aspect of repose; and, not careful to answer for herself, she commits her cause to Him who judges righteously. Even the intelligence of Christ's approach, after the death of her brother, produces, to appearance, little or no excitement. Martha, at the tidings, hastens to meet her Lord, while Mary sits still in the house till the Master calls for her.

On the whole, it is not the design of this sketch so to compare these two eminent women of the Scriptures, as to attempt any decision whatever in respect to the question which of them possessed the fairest, holiest character. He should be very cautious who would thus essay to bring forth their comparative merits. We shall perhaps be more wise should we view them as with their native differences, both of them evincing great excellencies of character, all of which are of great value, and all necessary to the perfection of society. Mary was contemplative; Martha was active. Mary was docile; Martha was inquisitive also. One of the apostles, when at their house, would have had no suspicion of coldness in

Mary; he would have been fully convinced of the cordiality of Martha. If he would have praised the quietness of Mary, he would have rejoiced equally in the vivacity of Martha. We love Mary as, at Simon's festival, she anointed the Messiah's sacred person. We equally love Martha as, at the same feast, she joyfully serves the table where the Messiah is feasting. We approve the quietness of Mary, as she waited at her house till Christ called her to witness her brother's resurrection. We, at the same time, honor Martha, who, in her earnestness, flies at once to the great Comforter, and, in her sprightliness, draws forth from his lips some of the most precious of Divine declarations touching the general resurrection. Mary's silence is impressive and beautiful; Martha's sociality is instructive and refreshing. We glance at Mary, and think of the eternal portion; we turn to Martha, and are reminded that activity to serve Christ is the sure means of gaining that prize. We need Mary—we cannot dispense with Martha. Remove the one, and we shall wander in pensive sorrow to find her; take away the other, and life's woes are at once redoubled. We love Martha—we love Mary. So did One other: "Now Jesus loved Martha and her sister."

Herodias.

ANOTHER Jezebel! But we must record her execrable name. She was grand-daughter of Herod the Great, and niece of the two Herods, Philip and Antipas. She was married to her uncle Philip; and Salome, the famous dancer, was their daughter. She afterwards forsook her husband, and married his brother, Herod Antipas, tetrarch of Galilee. This disgraceful connection took place, it is probable, about A. D. 33, and brought upon Herod and Herodias the righteous admonitions of John the Baptist. At the faithfulness of the man of God the guilty pair were deeply offended. It appears quite doubtful, however, that Herod would have proceeded to extremities with the Baptist. The latter, it is true, had displeased him; while yet, as Luke informs us, Herod feared John, and knew him to be a just and holy man, and even listened to him with pleasure; regarding, in his conduct, many of the instructions which he had received from him. Acting by himself, there seems but slight evidence that he would have interfered at all with the life, or even the liberty of the man, for whom he obviously felt a very high respect.

Hence, when John was incarcerated at the command of Herod, it was not so much to gratify any vengeance of his own, but it was "for Herodias' sake." The fearless preacher had pronounced her connection with Antipas, while her husband was living, to be unlawful. "Therefore," as the sacred historian proceeds, "Herodias had a quarrel against him, and would have killed him, but she could not." And the difficulty lying in the way of the murder was the above-named reverence of Herod for one whom he knew, and whom Herodias equally knew, to be a righteous man. As yet she had succeeded so far only as to procure from Herod his imprisonment. Such a punishment as this, however, was utterly unsatisfactory to this most hateful woman. Her bloody eyes were still fastened upon the innocent and noble minister of righteousness, and she crouched like a panther, waiting an opportunity to spring upon her imprisoned and helpless victim.

The fatal opportunity arrives hastily. Amid the festivities of Herod's birthday, the daughter of Herodias dances before him, and before the assembled grandees of Galilee. In his foolish admiration of her performance, the king promises, in the presence of the company, to give her whatever she should desire of him. The maid, consulting her mother touching the present to be asked, was directed to request the head of John the Baptist. Alas! what must have been the murderous and extreme hatred of this detestable woman! A very magnificent promise had been made to her daughter. She was encouraged, by her uncle, to request some gift that would enrich her for life. But, in the eyes of her mother, there could be nothing pleasant or desirable, so long as the hated Baptist was breathing. The opportunity she had so eagerly sought was presented. She well knew the great reluctance of the king. She had very obviously pressed her murderous measures before this time. Yet now, at last, had Herod committed himself, and he was caught in the snare that had been artfully laid to entrap him. And the great forerunner of the Messiah must bleed and die untimely, and when the brilliancy of his "burning and shining" career had just begun to flash before the eyes of startled multitudes.

Here comes the head! Open wide the palace doors, ye waiters;—and thou, executioner, pass in the charger. The dish is bloody, to be sure; and its contents are dreadful—very dreadful to behold; yet bring in the ghastly burden! Carry it, man of the axe,—carry it directly up to that charming damsel; it is her treasure. Now her fair and lily hands are reaching forth to take the dish. Be careful, butcher, that she holds it firmly. No matter for the blood upon those hands of hers; it is a fit emblem; and perchance they may be difficult to cleanse again. Bid her, as she bears it, to look steadily upon her gift, lest accident occur. She should gaze directly into those faded eyes; they are the gems which she preferred to half of Herod's kingdom. There, Salome! now move firmly. Carry that to your mother.

"Mother, the head is come!" Now, damsel, rest the charger upon that table; unclinch your slimy hands, and retire.

Draw near, vampire! Thy work is done—the blood is drawn—thy victim is prostrate. The silence is profound. From that clotted mouth no voice comes forth again to reprove thy lasciviousness. Those eyes seem gazing at thee, but it is only the death-stare, and they see not thy filthiness. Thy monitor sleeps his long sleep; and can any other voice disturb thy adulteries? Vengeance is glutted; and thou hast only added murder—keen, cold murder—to thy former foulness. Will there not be happiness as well as revelry now along those palace halls?

Little is known of the sequel of this bad woman. History tells indeed of her ambitious projects to advance her paramour and herself to loftier dignities—of her accompanying him to Rome, to aid his influence with the emperor for this object—the defeat of her hopes, through the agency of her brother Agrippa—her subsequent banishment with Herod to distant Spain, whence they never returned. What they suffered there—how long they lived—how they died, no man cares to inquire. Let their memory perish!

Salome.

We may give a passing notice to this child, who was, as we have seen, the daughter of the unfortunate Herod Philip, and the infamous Herodias. She appears to have accompanied her mother to the house of Antipas, while all that is related of her is in connection with the death of John the Baptist. The aspects of her character which are discernible from that brief and melancholy representation, are such as we might appropriately infer and expect. That she was an accomplished dancer, is plain from the inspired narrative. Of course, she had received an education in this, and, probably, other kindred accomplishments. From what is written of her, as well as from her rank, we may suppose her to have been long and carefully trained in those arts and graces whose end is to attract the admiration of the gay and licentious. Among other teachers engaged to perfect her in such a species of education, Herodias herself would naturally stand prominent. The whole process, indeed, had gone on under the supervision, and by the special directions of her mother. At the same time that mother, whatever may have been her external attractions, or intellectual capacities, ranked, as we know, among the most wicked and detestable of her sex. She was heartless— cruel—revengeful —shameless—impure—

ambitious, and, almost to the last degree, abominable. Her own gratification, at whatever expense of goodness and reputation—at whatever sacrifice of others' happiness, was the deity she worshiped. Such being her character, what would naturally be the impress she would make upon the daughter that grew up in her presence, and inhaled, from her infancy, an atmosphere thus polluted and ruinous? Was not this hapless child coming forth the sad counterpart of an abandoned mother's temperament and character? See we not here the baleful blossom presaging the forthcoming and bitter fruit?

But let us indulge a slight analysis. Salome danced enchantingly. "But is there any harm in dancing?" The writer is not careful to respond to this question. The history of this famous dancer supplies a sufficient answer. There was certainly harm—great harm, in the present instance. The beginning, truly, was beauty and rapture; but the ending was butchery, and death-struggles, and blackness of guilt too deep, almost, for grace to wipe away. "But it was an accidental, not a normal result." And is that so certain? Contemplate some of the circumstances of the dancer. Who and what are they who are the most forward in these scenes of amusements? Are ladies of genuine virtue and goodness particularly fond of the ball-room, and are they often seen there? What are the favorite hours of the dance? What of their dress, who seek prominence there? To be plain, is not the known result—and the *designed* result—an idolatrous admiration of the human form, and human gracefulness—the awakening of those passions of the heart whose undoubted tendency is to interfere with righteousness? Does not the dance contemplate some other things than virtue, and something inconsistent with virtue? And when, through the influence of the dance, moral goodness is prostrated, and evil passions begin to rise and triumph in the heart of a man, to what wicked extremities is he not ready to be drawn? He who knows not that from the dance—whether of the theatre, or the ball-room—the path is very straight to the "lusts that war against the soul," and that, from the lusts that war against the soul, the path is very straight to murder,—has, with all his knowledge, one lesson touching man's fallen nature yet to learn.

But what else of Salome? Her heart was steeled, and, to appearance, utterly insensible to virtuous sentiment and feeling. "What shall I ask, mother, of the king, who has promised to give me all my request?" What pleasant as well as innocent gratifications were now placed at her feet! How princely and magnificent was the offer which she received! Yet, receiving the directions from her bloody mother, it would appear that all was in keeping with her own disposition and taste. We hear of no surprise or disgust—no reluctance or hesitation. We can discern no distinction, in that girl's mind, between the head of a prophet murderously severed from his body, and a joint of butcher's meat just brought from the shambles. We look in vain to discern a single trace of virtue, humanity, or delicacy. She appears as if an imp suddenly sprung from the head of Apollyon, and as callous in respect to every refined, and generous, and virtuous sentiment, as if to her, wounds were smiles —and gushing blood were sport—and the blows of the death-ax, and the shrieks of the murdered, were delicious music. Fit progeny of such a parent!—a daughter, the detestable pander to the unnameable wickedness of a more detestable mother! Both the one and the other seem thrown a sickening blot upon the sex and upon the race; —a nauseous excrescence hanging out upon human society;—of an almost doubtful classification; human and terrestrial in form, satanic and infernal in genius.

Damsel! whose eyes shall glance along these pages, be assured of the reluctance of the writer to pain and sicken thee with even the briefest portraiture of the graceless, shameless Salome. It may, however, revive one sad, yet useful recollection; to wit, of what this nature of ours is capable. Viewing the maid that so coolly asked that a good man's head might be brought to her in a charger, and the mother who directed such a request from her child, let us assure ourselves anew of our mournful tendencies, and flee, as from the serpent, from whatever tends to indurate the sympathies of humanity, and deprave and poison the whole heart and character. Guard with watchful jealousy the fondness for what are termed fashionable accomplishments, and fashionable ornaments. Court not the admiration of the gay multitude. Care not to shine in splendors that must soon fade away forever, and to be the enchantress of circles where Christ is not welcomed, and where virtue and goodness too often weep and retire. Waste not thy golden hours and precious energies upon mere glitter and emptiness. Consider, rather, that for thee there is a loftier path, where purer airs await thee, and lovelier suns shall shine around thee, and every scenery shall charm thy spirit, and living fruits shall gladden and refresh thee by day and night. Walking there, thou shalt be greeted, on the right and on the left, by the excellent ones of earth. Intense and holy sympathy shall cheer thee upward, while, as life's terminus is approached, higher and purer beauty shall gild the scenery, until the nether paradise shall open into the everlasting kingdom.

The Syro-phenician Woman.

"A Minister of the circumcision" was Christ, so far as his personal ministry was concerned; and though he came to be a light to lighten the Gentiles, as well as the glory of his people Israel, yet it was not by his bodily presence in all nations that he intended to be for salvation to the ends of the earth. Hence, we hardly find Christ, in his brief ministry on earth, traveling beyond the limits of Canaan. On one occasion, however, he seems to have visited Phenicia; and, perhaps, for the very purpose of affording help in the one instance named, and to give to the Church of all coming ages so brilliant an example of genuine faith. Having come to the confines of that country, and granted help to the distressed woman, he immediately returned toward the sea of Galilee.

What had been the previous history of the woman of Canaan, we are not told. We may safely suppose, however, that she had either seen Christ, or had heard of him before his present visit to those parts, inasmuch as her whole conduct corresponds with such a hypothesis. It will be borne in mind that Capernaum and Bethsaida were not more than fifty miles from where Christ met this woman; and it will be remembered, also, that it was but a short time since, in those places, great wonders had been wrought by his hands. Nor can it be conceived as possible, that the tidings of these things should not have overspread the neighboring country of Phenicia. Had not this good woman heard of the wonderful cure of the Centurion's servant in Capernaum? Had she not heard of the healing of Peter's mother-in-law at the touch of Jesus? And had she not heard of his casting out the spirits with his word, and healing all that were sick? These, and similar mighty works, had been performed within a few miles of her own country, and within a few months of the day she met the great Physician. And in reference to these works he had declared, that had they been done in Tyre and Sidon—in the land where dwelt this "woman of Canaan,"—the inhabitants there would have repented in sackcloth and ashes. Nor had Jesus confined himself to the vicinity of the Sea of Galilee. By one of those sentences of Scripture which speak volumes, we ascertain that he went about all Galilee, (which borders upon "the coast of Tyre and Sidon,") teaching in their synagogues, and preaching the gospel of the kingdom, and healing all manner of sickness, and all manner of disease among the people. And his fame went throughout all Syria.

The Syro-phenician woman, then, had unquestionably heard of Christ; perhaps had seen him; and was already a firm believer in his power and mercy. He was now in the vicinity; and as she looked upon her poor, demoniac daughter, she, doubtless, revolved within herself whether this great Physician and Prophet, who had done so many wonderful things, and whose fame was all abroad, would not, if besought, help her, though a stranger and foreigner. At all events, she would venture the application. She could but fail; she might succeed. The case was one of extreme urgency; her child was "grievously vexed;" there was no repose by day or by night. Her dwelling was always frightful; the piercing cry of the insane was there, and the glare of madness was upon eyes which once looked upon that mother with filial and sweet affection. Hope seemed rapidly dying out of that sorrow-stricken heart, and she was perchance already wishing that her desolate one was laid away amid the still repose of the grave. There the wicked cease from troubling; there the weary be at rest, nor hear they the voice of the oppressor.

"But I will go for once and seek His aid, of whose goodness and power I have heard so much." Thus we seem to hear her exclaim; and she is hastening to Jesus, and her cries are already falling upon his ear. "Have mercy on me, O Lord, thou son of David!" Mercy is her plea—mercy for her daughter, and thus for herself—mercy, not from man, but from the Messiah. "Son of David!" This was her mighty argument; her appeal was to the great Anointed Restorer. Too great was he felt to be that she should presume to approach too closely, and her cry is from a distance.

He passes on his way, as though no voice was there, and still the cry of agony comes pealing on the ear. And all the while that soul burdened with pity was listening to the poor stranger, though she knew it not. Despair not, ye pensive ones, when, breathing your prayer toward heaven, there may seem to be no access—no listening—no care for you. Meanwhile, each softest complaint is heard, and every wish of yours interests the heart of Jesus. Murmur not if sometimes he tests your patience, your earnestness, and faith. "Send her away," say the disciples, "for she crieth after us." Nor in cruelty did they say thus. They asked not their Master to send her *empty* to her hapless home; but to send her thither as he had often done in other instances, with joy and rejoicing. "Send her away with the blessing she seeks!" was the prayer of that company. He spoke now; but cold seemed his answer, and distant, and repulsive. "I am not sent to her, but only to Israel's lost sheep." Whether she heard this chilling response seems not certain, though probable. She was, by this time, at hand, and the words just fallen from the Redeemer's lips appear designed for her ear, rather than for those to whom they were addressed. And now, in her agony, she is prostrate at the feet of the Deliverer, and again her cry arises, "Lord, help me!" Forbidding and dismal to that heart of sorrow were his former words; yet her suit was urgent. How could she go back to that melancholy home with no help! He had relieved others in happy multitudes. He had power to help her; and he was her last hope. Jesus speaks again; but they are cutting, lacerating words. True, they amount not to an absolute negative. He does not precisely respond, "I have no blessing for thee!" That would have gathered the damps of despair densely over the unhappy suppliant. Yet the words she heard could seem to afford but a struggling ray of hope, as he replied, "It is not meet to take the children's bread, and cast it to dogs." Was she not stunned at this cheerless reply? As the Master spoke thus, and the company was listening there, and the sobbing woman was fallen prostrate upon the earth, seemed it not, save to herself and to One other, that all was lost? Will she speak again? "Truth, Lord; yet the dogs eat the crumbs which fall from their master's table!" Thus she speaks; speaks thus to the perfect admiration of all that ever glanced at this incident of her history. Who has ever heard of anything beyond this in all the story of human intercessions? Profound respect and reverence are here joined, as is natural, with perfect humility and modesty. "Truth, Lord!" She worships the Saviour;—worships in deepest self-abasement. Wonderful aptness and judgment are here; and the retort is as capital and just, as it is, under the circumstances, impressive and affecting. Above all, mighty faith is here. It is as if we heard her exclaiming, "It is all as thou, Jesus, sayest. This poor suppliant is not among the children. She is, in the comparison, as a dog—the name which thy lips have given me, and which name itself will insure to me thy blessing; for the dogs under the table eat of the children's crumbs. At thy word, I am the dog under the table, and hence, a crumb is certainly for me."

Amazing triumph! The Infinite is conquered now, and can hold out no more. That cold severity retires at once from the countenance of the "Son of David," as when some dark cloud passes, all suddenly, from an autumn sun. Words, tender and beautiful as angels use, succeed to such as seemed so repulsive and freezing. "Great is thy faith—thy prayer is heard—the demon is gone!"

Pleasant that day to the "woman of Canaan," was her return from the field of conflict. Bloodless and innocent had been the victory she gained, like that of the ancient wrestler, at daybreak, on the banks of the Jabbok. Blessed, as she entered her doors, was the change that had passed over her once wretched home. Satan, with the speed of lightning, had been driven thence—the last shriek of the maniac had ceased its wild echoings; and sunny peace, in soft whispers, was breathing through those halls. Tremblingly she enters, and her heart swelling with untold emotions, she seeks the child of her affections. Within the chamber, reposing upon her couch in quietness, that child is found—her brilliant eyes falling, as she enters, upon her dearest mother. Long tost, and driven and lashed, as amid the wild billows of a boiling, frightful, and shoreless sea, where, above, lurid fires glared from sky to sky, and hideous spectres were flitting across her vision, and the horrid laugh of demons sickened her whirling brain, she had, all suddenly, heard a voice new, and of loveliness unutterable, hushing to peace. Then, in a twinkling, she was standing upon the solid earth, and looking aloft, the glorious sun lay deep in the far-spreading azure—and every sight and sound were only beautiful—and a soft hand seemed laid upon her disheveled tresses, composing to delightful tranquillity and healthfulness her agitated and tortured being. The transport, so sudden—so complete, had well nigh overcome her strength, and she had sought her couch, there to indulge her gushing tears of joy, and praise the Hand that stooped to bless a child; and there she waited the coming of her happy mother.

In after days, did they not often think of Jesus, and speak of him? Was not the "great faith" of the mother still greater now, and her love more elevated and intense? And that daughter, was she not, in the best sense, clothed, and in her right mind? And from these kindred hearts, arose there not the frequent song of praise and thanksgiving,—until they passed, both of them, away to where she who humbled herself to beg for "a crumb," found eternal plenty!

Mother! Is thy daughter as yet unrenewed, and her heart drawn away by evil and downward influences? Does the spirit of a sinful world still enthrone itself within her heart? And seems she fondly lured away by the hopes and vanities of a brief and uncertain life, and averse to the rational and lofty pursuit of holiness and heaven? The example of the woman of Canaan is given thee for thy instruction and encouragement. Like her, go, in behalf of thy daughter, directly to the great and compassionate Redeemer. Seek after and cherish "great faith" in his promises and mercy. Exercise a perseverance, such as is obstinate and unyielding; cultivate profound humility—begging, if it might be, but a crumb from his infinite fullness. And while thou prayest, bear always before thy child the spirit corresponding to thy prayers. Putting away all wrath, and clamor, and evil-speaking, talk often and skillfully of the things of Christ. Be his love always a familiar theme. Let everything pertaining to thy house be such as shall tend to invite the Saviour's presence and power. So shall that presence and that power dwell with thee, banishing evil spirits and poisonous influences, and fitting thee and thine for endless happiness and heaven.

Mother of James and John.

"THE mother of Zebedee's children" is several times mentioned in the evangelical history. From a comparison of Matthew xxvii, 56, with Mark xv, 40, it would appear very probable that her name was *Salome*. She was, in all probability, specially beloved by Christ. She doubtless entertained him often in Capernaum, and was one of the women specially designated as ministering to his wants in Galilee and other places. She was one of the celebrated women that were not content to see Christ, and hear him, as in his travels he passed their homes. At times we find her abroad, listening to the words of the Saviour; and in his last and dreadful agony, she was one of the weeping witnesses of his crucifixion. At the side of Mary Magdalene, and "the other Mary," stood the faithful Salome, looking on afar off, as they crucified the Lord of glory. She looked upon that dreadful scene, and was a spectator of the awful signs that accompanied the dying of the Son of God. So also was she associated with the Marys in the preparations for embalming the sacred body. She proved herself one of his most devoted and constant friends—lingering near him to the last, and yielding the last service within her power to proffer him.

One shade, however, rests upon the mother of

Zebedee's children, and which seems inseparably associated with her name. The Jewish idea of a temporal Messiah, and of great temporal prosperity and power under his reign, seems never to have been eradicated from the minds of the apostles, even to the day of Christ's ascension to heaven. On that very morning, as they assembled around their Master, they inquired whether he would now restore again the kingdom to Israel. They appear to have advanced but by slow degrees to the true idea of Christ's kingdom; and came not to the knowledge of the whole truth on this important subject until the ascension of the Lord, and the outpouring of the Spirit that soon followed.

It was with this idea of a temporal reign, that the sons of Zebedee petitioned for the most honorable places under the new order of things. We are surprised, in contemplating the ambition of these brothers, as well as the apparent boldness and imprudence with which they pushed their request. That their proceedings in this matter must produce the effect upon their brethren which was actually produced, might have been foreseen by a child, and could not have been unanticipated by the petitioners. A species of recklessness, therefore, appears to have accompanied their ungraceful ambition; while the whole affair is to be numbered among the most inexplicable circumstances of the apostolic history. The employment of their mother as their advocate in this case, may be accounted for, perhaps, from the probable fact of her great influence. We have seen her to have been one of the most faithful of all Christ's attendants who "ministered to his wants,"—and the sons naturally supposed that her intercessions would be specially availing in their behalf. It must be pronounced as being, on the part of James and John, a mean, weak, and altogether unfortunate transaction, and not at all in keeping with what we learn besides of the spirit and character both of the sons and the mother. And on the whole, how can we contemplate it otherwise than as one of those sad mistakes to which even very good people are exposed when at any time they dispense, even for a moment, with watchfulness and prayer? We may not doubt the general piety of the mother and her two sons; and they were specially distinguished by the Lord Jesus. It was much that *one* from a single family should be called to the apostleship. Much more was it that two brothers should at once receive this high distinction. It was more still, that both brothers should be recognized not only as apostles, but confidential friends of Christ. No family on earth was ever honored like that of Zebedee. No other mother could tell of two of her sons being both raised to the apostleship, and also to be two out of the three on whom the great Master, for reasons known to himself, bestowed special intimacy. All this may possibly help to account for the kindling of their unhallowed ambition, and the indiscreet proceeding to which it gave existence. Christ had greatly exalted the whole family. The result should have been their abounding gratitude and profound humility. But being, in this instance, unduly lifted up, they were left to unwise and shallow conduct, and to incur merited reproach. So true is it, that while humility is the forerunner of elevation, he that exalteth himself shall be abased.

Should some Christian mother, therefore, read this sketch,—some mother whose son has been called to God's holy ministry,—perhaps it may remind her to wish for that son, not that he may be accounted greatest and most renowned among his brethren. It will, I hope, be suggested to her to pray, rather that he may be divested of all pride and vain ambition; that he may, in his heart, lie at the feet of all his brethren—that the eminence he shall seek on earth shall be that of lofty devotion to Christ Jesus, and of far-spreading usefulness in his generation—that every faculty of his be consecrated to salvation. And if these things be so, that mother may dismiss her fears and rejoice. She shall see her son in great renown, one day—when "they that be wise, shall shine as the brightness of the firmanent; and they that turn many to righteousness, as the stars forever and ever."

Mary Magdalene.

LITTLE is known of Mary Magdalene. Her place of birth and residence was probably Magdala, of Galilee; and she had been one of the victims of demoniacal possession, and one of the multitudes of these afflicted ones who had sought and obtained relief from the Saviour's almighty hand. Nothing that was more disreputable than the affliction alluded to can be shown to have been associated with her name and character; and the various suspicions in which many have been pleased to indulge themselves concerning this excellent lady, are as unjust to her as they are indicative of the ignorance or carelessness of such as have been disposed to cherish them. It appears likely that Mary Magdalene, as well in character as in circumstances, possessed an unspotted reputation, and an elevated standing in society. Her whole attitude toward her adorable Saviour appears amiable and beautiful in the highest degree. She scarcely makes her appearance on the evangelical page, save in connection with the crucifixion and resurrection of the "Lord of glory." We observe her prominent among other women in witnessing his sufferings upon the cross. She was one of the weeping ones who followed him bearing his cross up the "dolorous pathway," and to whom he said, "Daughters of Jerusalem, weep not for me!" She was at the side of the disconsolate Mary when those words of the expiring Redeemer fell on the ear of John, saying, "Behold thy mother!" She was present when Joseph, the good and just, deposited the sacred remains within the sepulchre, and she beheld the arrangements, and how the body was laid. Of all the friends of Jesus she was the first who revisited the sepulchre on the morning of the resurrection; and was the first of human beings that discovered and gave information of the mysterious absence of the Saviour's body. Returning to the place of burial, she it was who stood weeping there, and as she wept, looked within the sepulchre and saw the two angels robed in white, and heard their heavenly voices. She it was who, before all others, saw the risen Christ. "Mary!" said the Lord of Life. "Master!" responded the astonished disciple. She it was who, first of all, was commanded to proclaim her Saviour's resurrection, and that his ascension on high was at hand. And "Mary Magdalene came and told the disciples that she had seen the Lord, and that he had spoken these things unto her." The apostles proclaimed to the world the resurrection of Christ; Mary proclaimed this resurrection to the apostles. If Paul was the "last of all," Mary was the earliest of all, to see the risen Lord.

Such was Mary Magdalene. Only a scene or two opens upon us in which she appears and acts.

Yet these suffice to indicate to us that she was one of the most devoted of all the Saviour's devoted followers, and one of the most excellent of women. During the ministry of her Lord and Master she was one of those who "ministered unto him of their substance." During his humiliation and passion she never left him for a moment. Of all his deep sufferings at the last she was a partaker, and was present and heard when he cried, "It is finished!" She "saw where he was laid" within the sepulchre, and prepared the spices and ointments for his body. She did what she could; and none of sacred women rise on the view, clad in fairer beauty and more becoming gracefulness than Mary of Magdala.

Sapphira.

THE story of Sapphira and her husband is one of deep and painful melancholy. They were both, as is probable, among the disciples; but of their origin, residence, or other circumstances of their history, the sacred record is silent. They rise before us only that we may contemplate their disastrous end, and the mournful cause that was concerned in bringing it to pass. Sapphira was obviously implicated entirely with her husband in the guilty transaction that proved their ruin. They were both concerned in the sale of the estate. When her husband retained a part of the price, Sapphira was privy to it, and consented to the measure. Alas for that act! There she fell, and there it was that loveliness and goodness departed hence. Her heart had yielded to crime, and her lie to Peter was the expression and sealing of her wickedness; and God cursed her with her husband, and the grave all suddenly closed over them both.

Sapphira lied. It is not narrated to us that this was her character. We are impressed rather that such was not her habit,—that in ordinary circumstances she was a truthful woman. In the present instance covetousness interfered—Satan was at hand to take advantage of the corrupt motions of nature—what faith she had gave way, and she sank. Great and terrible is the crushing and the wreck, when a soul, heretofore upright, deliberately consents to deception and falsehood. It is as when some beautiful edifice, reposing gracefully upon its foundations, falls instantly, by some dire convulsion, into a mass of shattered and sightless ruins. It is as when the brilliant and mighty engine leaps in its flight upon some deadly obstacle; there is the crash, the shock, the wreck, and the dying. Or it is as when some tall and noble ship—a few moments since, riding triumphantly over the billows—now smitten by some woeful disaster, goes down at once, beneath the cold and bottomless sea. When a man consents to falsehood—when he becomes guilty of a lie, then all is lost. If he has up to that time retained his integrity, he is conscious now of an infinite descent. He has taken a frightful leap. He has bidden adieu to goodness, purity, honor, rectitude, virtue. Heaven is veiled in blackness, and awful thunders alone meet his ear; if perchance he ever afterwards listens towards the eternal throne, a sickening and mournful sense of self-degradation comes over him. No external preacher or voice is necessary to convince him that he is fallen. A terrible monitor within is beating the funeral knell of his virtue and his happiness. If there be uprightness and innocence on earth, he knows full well that he belongs not among those elevated circles. Nay, even the dog of the street appears less degraded, and less hateful than he. That one lie still upon his conscience and character, and yet unwashed away, he will no more rise to goodness and to peace. He will remain a moral wreck. He may still sink—he will never ascend. God may not strike him literally and suddenly dead; but he has struck his own virtue to death, and has fatally poisoned the last sweet for the sake of which existence is desirable.

No warning can be too strong that we may deter the young of either sex from consenting ever, and by any means or mode, to the great and foul sin of falsehood. That this is a crime of special hatefulness, is sufficiently clear from the terrible retribution that met the hapless Sapphira, and her husband. Partners in falsehood, they were partners, the same day, in an untimely grave. The Lord slew them—slew them for lying! After this will one ever venture upon this melancholy ground? Will one venture even the slightest approximation? Shall it be absent, for any moment, from the mind, that lying stands recorded on the inspired page among the dark catalogue of transgressions that infallibly exclude the guilty one from the everlasting kingdom. "For there shall in no wise enter into it anything that defileth—neither whatsoever worketh abomination, or maketh a lie."

Dorcas,

"This woman was full of good works and almsdeeds which she did." What a beautiful testimonial is this to go down to all generations! How preferable to all monuments of marble, and all the proud memorials of fame and greatness! Far preferable even to the worship paid to learning and genius is a celebrity like this. Yet who believes it? Who discerns that to be greatly good and beneficent is the supreme end of life, and the highest elevation to be attained on earth?

Dorcas was distinguished by *good works.* Such were the operations of her hands. She wrought not evil, but good. Actions and efforts that were worthy, pure, benevolent, and lovely, emanated from her. She liberally clothed the naked. "Coats and garments" were by her, the products of her industry, with which to warm and comfort needy and suffering ones.

Nor was she limited to any one species of well-doing. She gave alms of such things as she possessed, whether of garments or other matters suitable for the relief of the destitute. Charitable objects were much upon her mind and heart, and she was disposed to bless in any mode which her means and strength would allow.

And she was *full* of these heavenly charities. They were not occasional with her. They were not spasmodic ebullitions of kindness. Her good works were a full and everflowing stream,—overflowing its banks and fertilizing the neighboring regions. She lived to do good. This was felt to be her calling—this was her occupation. Her own wants were comparatively few. She did not feel herself called upon to devote her time and energies to superfluities of dress, or luxuries of food. Many things in which most Christians indulge would have been agreeable to her likewise; but she could deny herself of these, and by such self-denial increase her means and measure of usefulness. And she preferred the luxury of doing good to all worldly enjoyments, and realized in her experience that it is more blessed to give than to receive. Many, doubtless, wondered at her course and manner of life. Some thought her righteous overmuch—and others fancied, perhaps, that more attention was due to her own worldly interest and affairs. But she had a loftier vision, and keener perception, and a purer faith. Other ladies were admired for their beauty, their wit, and other and varied accomplishments; but the blessing of such as were ready to perish fell upon Dorcas, while beams of life and love, emanating from her, animated and cheered their fainting hearts. Other ladies were admired—she was beloved. Others might be solicitous for themselves—she cared for the poor. Others might have pined over their own sorrows—she wept for the distresses of her neighbors. Others might have labored to escape the ills of life—she passed her days and years in drying up those ills, and subtracting from the number of human tears. She had no time for backbiting, tale-bearing, or mischief-making of any sort. Every influence going out from her was comforting, pure, and beneficent.

Hence she was good of heart. Christ has given us permission to estimate a tree by its fruit—a rule, by the way, too lightly esteemed in this age of creeds and parties. Yet it is by this same rule that we all judge Dorcas. She abounded in good works. These were the fruits; then the tree was good. The streams were sweet and refreshing; then the fountain was pure. We may assign her a place among the selectest spirits of this lower world. She had been translated out of the kingdom of nature into that of God's dear Son. She was a new creature. Christ had substituted in her heart benevolence for selfishness—life for inertness—faith for sight—fire for coldness—beauty for ashes—light for darkness. She had not originally an angel's nature; she wore not an angel's form; yet had she come to possess an angel's spirit and temper, and in her character was much more nearly related to heaven than to earth. It is difficult to imagine a stronger contrast than between Dorcas and some other female characters noticed in the Scriptures. Place her aside of Jezebel or Herodias, and who is not filled with wonder that beings so utterly diverse can be of the same race? Who exults not in his astonishment at the sublime triumph of grace, thus effectuating a moral change in man such as is scarcely less than infinite?

But Dorcas, the good and beautiful, sickened and died. Alas! who can escape that dreaded crisis? Who shall be discharged from that war? It would seem that if any one might escape, Dorcas might; so good was she—so benevolent—so useful—so beloved. But she slept; and seemed to sleep untimely,—drooped and fainted in the high day of her beneficent and brilliant energies,—

"Ceasing at once to work and live."

And they laid away her body in an upper chamber—laid it, as was meet, amid the memorials of her benevolent industry. Is it too farfetched that this should remind us of another scenery, when, away in the repose of eternity, good men shall one day be resting amid the loved fruits of godly labors on earth? Blessed are they that rest from their labors, and *their works follow them.*

But the death of Dorcas, so apparently disastrous, was with the Lord. He knew what He would do. "Parts of his ways" we may sometimes discern, and in the lamented death and sudden resurrection of this eminent lady, God was not without his designs of mercy; for it was known throughout all Joppa. She who had so fully honored Christ in her life and character, was admitted to the high privilege of being made a subject of his resurrection power before the eyes of multitudes who knew her; of whom many, as they saw the sight, believed in the Lord. In her life, she was an instrument of many temporal blessings and comforts; in her death and her recall, she was the occasion of a great turning to the Lord.

Lydia, Priscilla, Phebe, Tryphena, Tryphosa, Persis.

At the head of this chapter is written a cluster of names standing on the New Testament pages, and written in the book of life. They were holy women—friends of the apostle Paul—and helpers, in their sphere, in the great work to which he dedicated his vast energies.

Lydia, "whose heart the Lord opened that she

attended to the things which were spoken of Paul," became, under his preaching, a convert to Christ. Hence we wonder not that her doors were thrown open for the entertainment of the Apostle during his stay at Philippi; nor are we surprised at the earnestness and warmth with which she urged him to accept her Christian hospitalities. Well, it was a privilege indeed, when one might welcome within their dwelling an apostle of the Lord Jesus. And yet a greater privilege is ours, if the Master himself will come to us and take up his abode with us, and forever animate us with his spirit and his life.

Priscilla was another of the privileged ones that was permitted to entertain, in her house, the Apostle of the Gentiles. Paul first found her and her husband at Corinth, they having been directed by Claudius to depart, with other Jews, from the city of Rome. They accompanied the Apostle to Ephesus, where, after a time, they appear to have returned again to Rome. While they were at Ephesus, and after Paul departed from that city, Apollos, an eloquent man, and mighty in the Scriptures, arrived. Being not yet fully initiated into the dispensation of the Spirit, Aquila and Priscilla, when they had heard him, "took him unto them, and expounded to him the way of God more perfectly." A beautiful picture this! Apollos was mighty in the Scriptures—fervent in spirit—eloquent in speech—teaching diligently the things of God—being instructed in the way of the Lord so far as to the baptism of John. Yet it remained for Priscilla and her husband to introduce this eminent man to a more accurate knowledge of the Gospel—to enlighten him in respect to the full dispensation of the Spirit, which, since the day of Pentecost, had been granted to the world.

Happy are those pious women who, by their diligence and faithfulness in the things of God, become competent to give important instructions, even to able ministers of the gospel. Priscilla's experience had been conversant with a higher baptism than that of John, and to that higher baptism and experience was she instrumental in leading the eloquent Apollos. He could teach her in most respects, as a Jew—as concerning the Old Testament Scriptures—as far as to the extent of John's ministry, Apollos was much her superior; but as touching the way which "exceeded in glory," she was the superior of Apollos, and became his instructress and helper.*

Phebe, also, is to be classed in the holy sisterhood. Beautiful things are written of her by the apostle's pen. He styles her a servant of the church at Cenchrea—a sister beloved—a succorer of many others, as well as of himself, and commends her to the Christian sympathies and

* "There are many of the humblest babes of faith in corners of obscurity here and there, who really know more, and have a truer science of God, than some who are most distinguished among the Christian doctors."—*Dr. Bushnell on "Dogma and Spirit."*

aid of the Roman Christians, whom, for some reason, she appears to have visited.

"A succorer of many." Eminent commendation—excellent character! We ask no more. We place her at once aside the beautiful Dorcas, and think of her as one of the angels in human shape that walk this earth, soothing myriads of sorrows, charming away sickness, staying up sinking hearts and hands that hang down, putting to flight despondencies, waking a thousand smiles and joys, and gladdening life's shadows with perpetual gleams of holy sunshine.

Tryphena and *Tryphosa,* likewise, receive the salutations of the apostle, accompanied with the pleasant commendation that they were laborers in the Lord.

The beloved *Persis,* too, "labored much in the Lord."

These holy women were not idle disciples. There was a sphere of action in which they could with propriety move, and thus they became important "helpers" in promoting the great cause of salvation. They were not spectators, fault-finders, drones; they were among the most efficient laborers in the same cause in which the apostles were employed. They knew the way of the Lord, and were capable of instructing others, and of aiding them to enter and walk in the same highway of holiness.

⁂ Having noticed in the preceding pages certain specific and prominent females brought to view in the Holy Scriptures, it remains that we conclude our sketches with a brief analysis of two or three abstract characters alluded to on the inspired page.

The Fretful Woman.

SUCH a woman is named in the sacred writings, and her description is nearly what follows.

She brawls. She opens her mouth wide, and her voice is harsh and shrill, and is heard afar, and passes without, and agitates the streets. It is a coarse voice, for it is a coarse and low mind that is roaring through it. When she performs, all the house rings again, from foundation to garret; so that, should the confounded husband attempt to seek refuge in the housetop, and in the corner thereof,—according to the suggestion of the wise man,—he would, by no means, escape the amazing sound.

She contends. It is true, woman should be slow to dispute; and she, especially, should leave off contention before it be meddled with. Yet the fretful woman has never learned effectually this great lesson. She is contentious, and even against the one with whom a wise woman will scarcely ever dispute—her own husband. In her strife of words, she knows how to yield nothing, save all her attractiveness and power. She seems to deem the "last word" of more importance than the respect and affection of her husband, or the peace of her family; and the last word she will have.

She is often angry—as a matter of certain consequence. When a woman contends, and her voice is loud and harsh, we may expect a miracle as reasonably as the absence of anger. She becomes inflamed. Her wrath aggravates the grating tenor of her voice, and the latter again blows up the rising flames of anger and of rage, and the speech becomes rapid as well as clamorous; violent gestures accompany; the face becomes flushed; the eye wild and fiery; the aspect menacing and frightful; love, beauty, sweetness, grace, all are flown; while the astonished husband stands aghast at the contrast between the object before him, and the fair being he used to love so well.

Yet all this might not be utterly ruinous, if the storms were seldom; but the unerring pen writes that the contentions of a wife are a continual dropping, aye, a continual dropping in a very rainy day. The region is desolate where this poor woman moves, and frets, and scolds. Transient and doubtful are the gleams of sunshine that struggle between the clouds. The thunders are often rolling; the wild storm-wind is often sweeping athwart the landscape, and its path is gloomy and desolate. Peace and prosperity come not there, and every lovely plant droops and fades.

"It is better to dwell in the wilderness than

with a contentious and angry woman;" so comfortless, so utterly cheerless, is the house and home where such a woman bears sway. Her husband is full of fears. He fears for his neighbors. Fain would he avoid that himself and his family should be a nuisance amid the circle where he dwells. He could, with greater fortitude, endure for himself; but he is distressed that the eruptions within his own habitation should send their echoings abroad to the disturbance of other families, or that of the strangers that pass peacefully through the street.

He fears for his wife. What becomes of her peace, her piety, her influence, her reputation, her health, her progress toward perfection?

He fears for his children. Alas! will they grow up peaceful and lovely amid these stormy and disastrous influences? Will they, save by extraordinary providence, be preserved from catching the dreadful infection with which their home is daily charged?

He fears and mourns for himself. It is not too much to say of him that he is a disappointed and unfortunate man. The truth of the proverb finds a deep and affecting response in his soul. He thinks of the "wilderness," and wishes himself there. If not strongly fortified by virtuous principle, no marvel if he seeks those haunts that are even more dreadful than the desert, and those companions that are more dangerous and more hateful than the beasts of prey.

The Proud Woman.

SHE is a lover of brilliant dress. She is not careful for the ornament of a meek and quiet spirit, which is, in the sight of God, of great price. She covets rather the outward adorning of plaiting the hair, and of wearing of gold, and the putting on of apparel. We read of the chains, the bracelets, the mufflers—of the head-bands, the ear-rings, the finger-rings—of mantles, and wimples, and crisping pins. Such was the blazonry of pride in the ancient days, and even among the daughters of Zion. And such it is in every age. The putting on of artificial ornaments is one of the prominent developments of this dreadful plague of the human heart. If there be beauty, it must be thus set off to the greatest imaginable advantage. If natural beauty be absent, a sort of factitious elegance must be secured by the aid of outward adorning. Thus it is that more than half of many precious lives is worse than wasted, and multitudes of hearts debased and corrupted.

She is haughty. Having an inordinate esteem for herself, she feels a corresponding disdain for others. There is a circle with which she deigns to associate; with the great multitude she has no sympathy, and for them she has no pleasant word —no smile of friendship—no sentiment of benevolence. These daughters, writes the prophet, "are haughty, and walk with stretched forth necks." Of lofty bearing are they, nor, as they pass, can they so much as turn to look upon their more humble fellow-traveler to the tomb.

She is selfish. It is *self* that she worships, adorns, pampers. Instead of esteeming others better than herself, she reverses that evangelical rule, and none is so high in her esteem and admiration as her own person. In her thoughts she stands first of her sex, while others, in the comparison, are lightly esteemed. For herself, and her own immediate circle, she is alone interested. Provided her own gratification and aggrandizement are secured, she feels very little concern for all the rest of the world. All the beautiful charities of piety are strangers to her narrow and callous heart. She would not dispense with one of her expensive dresses, or useless ornaments, to soothe a widow in her affliction, or save a weeping family from starvation. She lives for self, and for self alone.

She is ignorant. Esteeming herself as better than others, is she correct? Counting others as undeserving of her notice, is she not mistaken? Contemplating this transient life, as given to be devoted to ostentation and vanity, has she not her first lessons yet to learn? Absorbed in selfishness, and forgetful of the grave, is she not blind? Certainly there can be no surer evidence of ignorance the most deplorable than pride. The proud woman imagines that she is rich and increased in goods, and knoweth not that she is poor, and miserable, and wretched, and blind, and naked. The whole work of goodness and grace she has yet to study and learn. She is to put off her haughtiness, and become as a little child, and sit, with Mary, at Jesus' feet, and learn of him—all this she must yet do, if she shall ever enter into the kingdom of heaven.

She is ridiculous. What, in the clear eye of good sense, are many of the ornaments she puts on, and which she so highly values? What of that "stretched forth neck," those "wanton eyes," that "walking and mincing as she goes?" What of that self-esteem and self-adoration, too obvious to be concealed from the most superficial eye? And what of the supreme self-ignorance just alluded to? What would the proud woman say or think, were she assured that the ridicule of the multitude is fully equal to her own haughtiness? Hast thou never witnessed, within the refuges for the insane, a woman of lofty mien—of form strong, straight, and stiff—of pompous gait—and robed fantastically—and crowned withal—the self-imagined queen of some powerful state? And, as you looked, counted you the insane exhibition to be ridiculous? And yet, not half so much so was it, as the outgoings of pride in another woman, reckoned to be rational.

She is hateful. For pride is always hateful in either sex, and at any age of life; a stain upon the character, that is unseemly and disgusting.

There is an unreasonableness that is felt to the quick—a self-imagined superiority, which is as deformed as it is ridiculous, and with which the beholder has no sympathy. The folly involved is as intolerable as it is conspicuous; the hatefulness is that which is, to the last degree, offensive and sickening; the impure loftiness is that whose depression and humiliation relieves and refreshes our spirits, while it excites our pity.

In innumerable instances, pride has proved one of woman's greatest defects—the foundation of a large proportion of her faults and blemishes, and has spoiled, by its presence, a form and aspect that had otherwise been decidedly beautiful and attractive.

And the proud woman is doomed to disappointment and sorrow. Hateful as pride is in the eyes of man, it is even much more so to God; and, in his providence, is wont to be followed by mournful consequences. To him a proud look is offensive, and every one that is proud of heart is an abomination in his sight. Hence we read of his resisting the proud—of his knowing them afar off—of his not respecting them. And we read of his threatened judgments. The proud shall be abased—they shall be taken in their pride, and a fall is to succeed. Pride goes before destruction—it shall be marred—stained—brought down—wept over—scattered.

The Strange Woman.

She forgets God. God is not in all her thoughts. She is entirely estranged from Him who is the fountain of all purity, and who cannot look upon sin with the least degree of allowance. Her endeavor is to place God, and all thoughts of him, as far as possible from her mind, while she is emphatically of that class who are without God in the world. It is thus she prepares herself to work all wickedness with greediness. Cut off from God—from all fear and love toward him, what, in degradation, may not a human being become? Shut off the sun, and turn away amid utter darkness, into what dreadful pitfalls and frightful depths may we not fall?

She forsakes the guide of her youth. She was taught better lessons in the happy days of her childhood and early youth. The fear of the Lord was impressed upon her mind and heart. Instructions pure and beautiful were wont to fall upon her ear. A father's manly voice had taught her—a mother's deep affection had entreated her. And she once entered the house of God upon the holy Sabbath-day, and used to hear the holy commandment preached and enforced, and the blessed gospel breathing forth its invitation of boundless mercy. And there sometimes swept by her, as it had been sweet voices from another world, whispering of the beauties of holiness; and many an upward and sacred influence came to guide her youth to spiritual and immortal happiness. All that was lovely and good—whether on earth, or in purer and happier worlds—all pointed her away from the joys of sense and the pleasures of sin, and prompted her to lift her heart for a higher and holier destiny. Yet from every golden cord she has broken away—from every scene of innocence and beauty she has retired. From all elevated and lovely circles, she has gone down. The guide of her youth is forsaken—and far off the wanderer strays—and her feet are treading near to the dead—and her steps take hold on hell.

She is clothed with the harlot's attire. The costume appropriate to innocence and virtue accords neither with her taste, nor with the purposes of her heart. She covets not the robes with which truth, and beauty, and goodness delight to deck themselves. She adorns herself rather that she may, in her subtilty, ensnare the wandering eye, and the frail, unguarded heart.

She is without in the streets. What knows she of the joys of *home*—the true and noble delights of the family circle? A husband's smile—the sweet simplicity of childhood—virtuous occupations—instructive books—refreshing converse—holy love—what are all these to her? That mind is debased; that heart is withered; and all the glory has departed; and she knows no home save the excitement and the whirlpool of sin.

How can she linger in the presence of virtue? Or how can she endure the company of her own dark thoughts? She is abroad; and especially "in the twilight." The evening shades are more favorable to her purposes. The destroyer that approaches us will choose darkness rather than light, for his deeds are evil.

She is cruel. She seeks only evil, and no good. Her aim is not to save, but to ruin. She promises, indeed, present joy, but her end is bitter as wormwood—sharp as a two-edged sword. Straying far away from the path of life herself, she would lure others to accompany her, as her feet go down to death. She reacheth forth her arms to embrace her victim, but it is the embrace of destruction.

She watches for her prey. Her eyes are open, as she is abroad in the streets, and she lieth in wait at every corner. She is subtle of heart, and cunning in that knowledge which is death, rather than life. Her wandering yet observant eye is scanning the passing multitude, and is keen to detect its prey. There he comes; a youth, one of the simple ones, and void of understanding. Through the street he is coming, and he approaches near where she waits to deceive. Her evil and practiced eye discerns at once. His dress; his gait; the airs he assumes, all mark him as the victim—alas, the *willing* victim! Happy, had he been elsewhere amid "the dark night;" or if there, it was a pity that his eye did not look right on, and his eyelids straight before him, and that, with the glad elasticity of youth, he had not hastened his footsteps to his room, his Bible, and his God!

She seduces. With varied and consummate art she allures and captures her object. There is the smile of apparent affection and interest; and there are the lips whose words of flattery drop as the honeycomb, and a voice which is smoother than oil. The fascinating glance—the ensnaring gesture—the soft invitation—are all there. Engaging professions and promises, it may be, are also there. "I came forth to meet thee—diligently to seek thy face, and here I find thee." With her much fair speech she causeth him to yield, and "he goeth after her!"

She destroys. The simple one, being taken in the snare of the strange woman, is ruined. If it be his first step downward, the second step follows almost of course. He has shot within the whirling basin of the awful Maelstrom, and his doom may be written as certain. As he goeth after her, it is as an ox goeth to the slaughter; till a dart strike through his liver; as a bird hasteth to the snare, and knoweth not that it is for his life. He is a wounded, bleeding man, cast down and slain, where many a strong man has fallen. But will he not rise again? Yes, by miracle—not ordinarily. They come not up from that disastrous ruin. For her house inclineth unto death, and her paths unto the dead. None that go unto her return again, neither take they hold of the paths of life. It is said that there is mourning at the last, when the flesh and the body are consumed. Her house is the way to hell, going down to the chambers of death.

She destroys herself. Her career of sin is transient, and seems but commenced, when it closes forever. Disease—her own disease—comes sternly, and almost certainly. Beauty and attractiveness rapidly wane away. Meanwhile, the heart is already dead. This world is hung in sackcloth; and the future is darker and more terrible still. Herself wicked, wicked ones surround her. God has withdrawn—heaven is closed—foul spirits are in attendance—and she dies in despair,—welcomed out of this world by her associates in crime—welcomed among the unclean and the lost—kindred beings, for whose companionship she hath prepared herself.

Daughter! come not thou into their secret;—to their hateful assembly be not thou united!

The Virtuous Woman.

She is of great price; of so much value as not to be compared with precious stones, silver and gold, houses and lands, or whatever riches the world can afford. For what is all the world, if she be absent? Or what of all other earthly losses, if she remain?

Her husband trusts her; trusts her without misgiving; trusts her with all his heart. Nor is his confidence betrayed. He trusts her safely. All the affairs of his house are managed with great economy and wisdom, so that he has no need of spoil; no need of invading the rights of others, either for his own support or gratification.

She will do good to her husband, without mixture of evil. Her words are pleasant words as he meets her at the table, in the parlor, or elsewhere. Her deeds are pleasant deeds, and such as conduce to her husband's happiness and welfare; while, by her goodness and prudence, she will give him no pain, and bring him no reproach or injury. Such will be her practice perpetually. The beauty of her conduct and character will gild her husband's years with unclouded sunshine.

She is provident, and prepares whatever may be necessary. Not careful for superfluities, all materials for necessity and comfort are, if possible, in her house; nor are her own hands idle in all the requisite duties of her family. And there is no reluctance. She suffers no caprice or discouragement to restrain her activity. Her efforts and movements are sprightly, and willing, and cheerful. Her heart accords with her judgment; and she has no clearer perception of what is proper in her house, than she has readiness and delight in her efforts to secure it.

To say of her that she is not idle, is frigid. She is of great industry. "She riseth while it is yet night." The day commences with the dawn, and it is a day of action—of decided, strong, and well-directed effort. She waits not for her duties to be suggested by another;—"she seeketh;"—her eye is intent upon what may be necessary or useful, and her powers go forth in constant and earnest industry. And those powers are strong and efficient. In the midst of her industry, and the high purposes of her mind and heart, she is awake, and animated, and joyous. No time has she for desponding, or weakness, or faltering, or murmuring. She appreciates the important position which she holds, as well as the duties that are appropriate, and "she girdeth her loins with strength, and strengtheneth her arms." Should reverses happen—as happen they will—she still keeps her eye upon the great God of providence—appropriates his promise—emerges above the billows—and prosecutes with vigor the works of her hands.

And the works of her hands are genuine and

excellent. "She perceiveth that her merchandise is good." Nothing marred, unseemly, defective, proceeds from her industry. The linen she makes is "fine linen;"—in other words, all her products are beautiful and good. A pure and lovely fountain is she, and the streams thereof are only sweet and refreshing streams.

She is of great enterprise. There is no meanness in her plans, nor in any of her arrangements or processes. She has the merchant's enterprise, and food from distant countries is seen, at suitable times, upon her table. For there may be piety, as well as gratification, in tasting the fruits of other climes; and every creature of God is good, and nothing to be refused, if it be received with thanksgiving.

She is farseeing. When there is necessity, she can plan for the future comfort of her family, as well as for present enjoyment. Hence, if any exigency require it, she is capable of negociating purchases, and of providing more ample domains —the fruit of her own industry and wisdom.

Thus, she is above want. Her house is comely and respectable. She is not afraid of the snows and storms of winter, for all her household are clothed in scarlet. They are clothed abundantly, in other words, and with appropriate neatness and elegance. And her food, from far and near, is laid up, and there is a sufficiency for all that comprise her household. The aged ones, if they be there—the maidens—the little children—the husband—all are duly and abundantly provided for.

Nor, amid her abundance, are the desolate and poor forgotten. Her virtuous heart is not encaged within her own doors. Providing well for her own household, her eye is abroad also in quest of suffering and sorrowing ones. For these too she has a portion. Nor does she wait for them to come to her—she seeks them out. "She stretcheth out her hand to the poor; yea, she reacheth forth her hands to the needy." As she moves amid the destitute and the suffering, her steps are as those of some bright angel of mercy, and the blessings of such as are ready to perish meet her as she goes.

She is benignant. When she speaks, it is with wisdom. Her voice is music;—there is no harshness nor bitterness; but "in her tongue is the law of kindness." She is a friend to all; she would do good to all; she will, if possible, give pain to none. Her smiles are abundant, and they are genial, like the reviving sunbeams, and waking along her pathway a thousand hopes, and cheering and blessing the heart of sadness. She is beautiful, amid the circles of her influence and usefulness, as the bright star of evening, and her name is precious as ointment poured forth.

For she is honorable; honorable at home; and, as a mother, "her children rise up and call her blessed." A blessing has she been to them beyond human computation. A part of her worth they see and appreciate, and pronounce their blessing upon her. Through her influence, in a great measure, they are coming forth upon the theatre of life, a pious, comely, and useful company, fitted to adorn the circles of earth, and promising to be flourishing and happy in the eternal sequel. "Her husband, also, and he praiseth her." She has been the greatest and best gift of earth to him—the solace and charm of his mortal existence; soothing his sorrows and enhancing every joy of his life, and essentially aiding, by her excellence of character and manners, his reputation and honor. A woman of another temper might have crushed his prospects and his hopes; but now he "is known in the gates when he sitteth among the elders of the land." He is the husband of "the virtuous woman," and she is honorable abroad—one of the selectest ornaments of her neighborhood—a woman that feareth the Lord, and "she shall be praised," for strength and honor are her clothing.

"A woman that feareth the Lord;" thence her high virtue and excellence. The Divine pen having written this one sentence, no further explanation is necessary. The fear of the Lord is the beginning of wisdom, and a good understanding have all they that do his commandments. The virtuous woman is a God-fearing woman. She sees him ever around her. She hears him in every passing breeze, and in every falling shower. His book lies open upon her table, and the words on which she ponders there, "they are spirit and they are life" to her soul. Her house—God reared it over her head; and those rooms, and all the beautiful and pleasant things that meet her there, God spread them out before her. Her husband—God placed him at her side, and her sons and daughters were gifts from heaven. Her health—her mind—her comfort—the bright sunshine of her life—God ordered all, and from him came down every good and perfect gift. Her sins—God has hidden them; her brilliant hopes—God has inspired them; her eternal mansion—God has erected it, somewhere in heaven. God, with her, is all, and in all. Toward him her spirit leans with unutterable longing—to him she is wedded in ineffable union—to please and glorify him is the burning passion of her soul—to offend him is the bitterness of death and woe to her heart—to be like him is the strong and incessant endeavor of her being—to participate in his eternal kingdom and praises, is her absorbing expectation and hope. To shut God from her mind and heart, would be like the setting of the sun behind the shadows of eternity, and the sickening eclipse of everlasting night. "Whom have I in heaven but thee, and there is none upon the earth that I desire besides thee," is poetry with which her soul knows infinite sympathy. She "feareth the Lord;" and it is a fear deep, inwrought, sanctifying, vivifying, abiding, saving. Here discern the virtue of the virtuous woman. Here mark the fountain whence issues every sweet and refreshing and gladdening stream.

No wonder, then, that we read of this woman, that "she shall rejoice in time to come." The virtuous woman, steadfast in her eminent virtue —what harm can befall her? She will pass on to age; but they will be years of honor—years of accumulated wisdom, love, happiness. As when one ascends far up some mountain-height, her prospect of beauty will be reaching wide and still wider into the distance. Lying down to die, the blessings of multitudes shall encircle her death-bed, and a voice from Eternity shall whisper, "Well done, good and faithful!" Retiring from earth, she will live on high, conspicuous and renowned among the many daughters that "have done virtuously."

THE END.

www.ingramcontent.com/pod-product-compliance
Lightning Source LLC
LaVergne TN
LVHW050531100826
845148LV00002B/516

* 9 7 8 1 4 2 5 5 1 9 3 8 4 *